Growi

with

Sensory Issues

Insider Tips from a Woman with Autism

Jennifer McIlwee Myers

Growing Up With Sensory Processing Disorder:
Insider Tips from a Woman with Autism

All marketing and publishing rights guaranteed to and reserved by:

721 W Abram St, Arlington, TX 76013

800-489-0727 (toll free)

817-277-0727 (local)

817-277-2270 (fax)

E-mail: *info@sensoryworld.com*

www.sensoryworld.com

© 2014 Jennifer McIlwee Myers

Cover and interior design, John Yacio III

All rights reserved.

Printed in the United States of America.

ISBN: 978-1-935567-44-8

Dedication

To Gary and also to Catherine, without whom …

Acknowledgments

There are so many people who have contributed information, time, and energy to this book that it's ridiculous. If this were the Academy Awards, I'd get played off before I could remember one-tenth of them. Actually, that would be great, because getting cut off early would give me an excuse for the fact that I cannot possibly get to everyone.

I've learned an amazing amount from folks I barely know or only met once from both the Sensory Processing Disorder community and the autism community. There are people who came up to me at conferences and shared everything from great advice to harrowing personal stories. Also, this one time, after I admitted during my talk that I carry a Lego Loki as one of my talismans, a woman came up to me and pulled a plush Thor doll out of her purse, and we made them fight.

A few of the specific people I can remember at the moment:

My parents, Roy and Ruth McIlwee, who were astonishingly intelligent and inventive when it came to creating ways to teach me to be a person. They are also under the parental delusion that I'm wonderful. Please, nobody tell them otherwise, they don't need to know.

My sister, Catherine, has taught me about strength and character and will deck me if she ever catches me wearing a scrunchy. She's just protective like that.

My brother, Jimmy, who is just plain great.

My nephew, Pete, didn't have a lot to do with this particular book, but since I'm really late getting him a birthday present I figure I've got to find a way to get back on his good side.

Cassie Zupke and her mad crew have (ironically) helped me stay sane. Google her, read her book, "Like" Cassie Zupke's Autism Blog on Facebook. More than worth it.

My friend HyeKyeung Seung, who taught me to hear new sounds.

Carol Stock Kranowitz, for being an endless source of inspiration and information about SPD. Another nut, by the way, but it seems all the best people are.

Lucy Jane Miller, PhD, much of the same as Carol in the way of inspiration and information, but even more so for her championing of SPD in research and of children with SPD every single day.

The Gilpins, including but not necessarily limited to Wayne, Jennifer, Kelly, and Alex. Without all of their help I might never have become a writer, and certainly would be less of a person.

Teresa Corey, for (usually) keeping me (almost) sane on the road.

The entire staff of Future Horizons and of Sensory World. These are publishers that outdo the others in a zillion ways, and I'm grateful to be a "kissin' cousin" to the FH/SW family.

I'd like to mention Kim and Annie and Sheri and Lyn specifically, but that wouldn't be entirely fair because I can't remember the names of everyone else at FH I want to thank right now.

All of my piano teachers and guitar teachers, who I will not name for fear people might associate their skill level with my lack of musical talent. They taught me a lot by stubbornly working with me even though I had no idea what I was doing.

My speech therapists. All of their names are faded now, but I remember each of them with smiles and an immense feeling of relief that they showed up and worked with me, week after week. They saved my bacon in even more ways than they knew.

I've had too much caffeine and too little sleep, so not only are there amazing people who haven't been mentioned here, the ones who are here haven't been thanked adequately.

Gary Myers. Because.

Table of Contents

S ince this isn't your typical book on Sensory Processing Disorder (SPD), I feel it is only fair to let you know what you are getting into. There are three major areas of weirdness you should definitely know about up front.

First: This book does not fit the typical SPD-book mold in some ways. A lot of books on sensory processing disorder offer really detailed explanations of how each individual sense is affected in each possible permutation of SPD, and provide a ton of checklists and generally provide a full overview of the diagnostic process as well as an overview on treatment possibilities and standards. These books are focused on getting parents educated about what SPD looks like from the outside and how they can find professionals to help their child. This is, absolutely, a great thing to have resources for. But it's not what I have to offer.

This book will spend some time discussing how important the sensory systems are to human functioning, and what the different categories of sensory processing disorder are called, what they are, and how they can trip up an unsuspecting child or adult. That should help get us all on the same page, so to speak.

But much, much more than that, this book is about what it is like to grow up with SPD. This is about being an unknowing SPuDster, trying to find ways to get through childhood, and hitting a ton of walls. This is about what helps and hurts when you are putting forth the best effort you know how to, and yet not able to get the information or support you need to succeed, especially in school.

This is about how my parents supported me by teaching me good life skills that helped me get by despite my limitations. It's about things that you wouldn't think of, things the average therapist wouldn't have time to discover that make life better, sweeter, and worth living even though you're the last kid picked for everything.

I think I may even have some info that will help parents, teachers, and therapists tell when they need to provide extra support or information. I am very much against "coddling" kids with SPD (or other disabilities). I am very much for providing growing kids and teens with the support they need to become more than Problem Kids or a kids with problems.

Second: This is a chatty, talky book. That means the style here is conversational. If you've heard me speak and read anything else I've written, you know that I write like I talk. Determining whether that's a good thing is outside of the scope of this book.

What's important is that many little things in this book would not be correct if I were writing a paper, essay, or a "real" book. That means I need to warn the grammar lovers that pronouns will be used in an eccentric way. English has no simple neutral pronoun that means "either he or she," so sometimes examples I will use "he," sometimes "she," and sometimes "they." "They" is the closest thing we've got to a neutral pronoun in this language, and I'm not afraid to use it. So if I say, "A child with sensory problems may feel they are all alone," please understand that this is simply how I generally speak of one person who may be either a he or a she. More importantly, DO NOT send hate mail to my editor. It's not her fault! Trust me, anyone who has to edit my prose has more on their plate than they can possibly handle.

Third: This is a book by a person with SPD. Not only do I have SPD, but I also have found that among the parents and families of children with SPD, there are many, many people who have some SPD traits.

In fact, if you add up the fact that SPD often seems to run in families with the way SPD quite often (though not always) comes in tandem with such things as ADHD, learning disabilities, and autism spectrum disorders, it is very likely that there are quite a few readers who are very much quirky, eccentric, and/or geeky like me. These people represent an audience that is in some ways underserved by the many, many books on SPD written by people who have followed a more typical developmental path.

Because I'm a nerd with SPD and because either my readers or the children with SPD they are dealing with may well be the same, there are important ways in which I will be working to support that audience. I will be as honest and even blunt as I can be when it comes to talking about the emotions and frustrations that so often come with SPD.

Also, I will be throwing in some nerdtastic references from time to time. There is a common geek culture that many of us with strong SPD traits share, and small fragments of it will surface from time to time here. Considering the vast number of books written by the non-geek population on this topic, and the vast number of references they make on the assumption that the readers are "typical" in their interests, it is only fair to have a few tiny moments when this book goes the other direction.

Don't worry if you're more the typically developing (not very weird) type of person – I will make sure that the text is clear whether or not you recognize those little "shout outs." Inclusivity and tolerance are important here.

So there you have it. This is not entirely the standard kind of book on SPD, the grammar is based on a casual everyday mode of speech rather than the typically grammatically correct written use of the language, and there are little things thrown in for the quirkier reader and (let's face it) because I love geek stuff. If you feel you can read under those conditions, please, come in and read a bit. Heck, if you don't feel so sure about it, why not give the book a shot anyway? While I'm asking you not to write hate mail to my poor, innocent editor, you can get on the Internet and complain to or about me all you like afterwards.

Last but not least, welcome to this book! Make yourself at home!

Getting Started

Who are we? Why are we here? No, I'm not going to address the big questions of life, the universe, and everything. I'm going to try to let you know why this book might be useful to you and whom and what it's for.

This book is written for humans: parents, teachers, therapists, and pretty much anyone else connected to someone with Sensory Processing Disorder (SPD)—or who want to know what SPD is. It's also for anyone who wants to understand SPD better and/or anyone who might want some practical examples for helping kids with SPD.

What should you expect from this book? Well, I'm going to be solidly frank with you folks who haven't experienced SPD from the inside. I'm not just going to provide directly helpful info, like examples and ideas, I'm *also* going to spend some serious time explaining what approaches are hurtful and what it means to a kid when the adults around her just don't "get it."

I'm assuming that if you have picked up this book, you have some ideas about what SPD is—and that you are dealing with an actual human being with SPD and want to be able to help him or her and figure out how to survive the process of growing up with SPD. The stories and ideas here mostly coalesce around childhood, but as an adult with SPD, I'll be sharing some stories from my recent experiences as well.

1

There is no age limit on either having SPD or improving one's sensory processing and outlook—seriously! Okay, there's one limit: Posthumous diagnosis doesn't actually help the person with sensory processing issues (but, sometimes looking back at late family members with a new understanding often actually makes the past clearer).

So, dear reader, whether you are a parent or a teacher, an occupational therapist (OT) or a pediatrician, there is something here for you. If you are simply stuck in the bathroom with nothing else to read, I'll do my best to produce some interesting stories and amusing factoids to provide you with a bit of entertainment.

To make a long story short, this book is intended for a pretty broad audience of people interested in learning about and coping with Sensory Processing Disorder. That's not just because my publisher would like a book that several people will actually buy—it's also because I like you. I really, really like you.

No, no, I'm not hitting on you. Having spoken around the United States to a lot of folks about sensory issues (and also autism and Asperger's Syndrome and anything else people will sit still for), I've found that I am really quite fond of people who want to learn and understand more. I'm just pleased to meet anyone who genuinely wants to be a better, more effective parent/teacher/therapist/person.

It's pretty darn great to deal with folks who want to learn—especially when they are going through a serious rough patch with a child who definitely did not get the factory-standard brain, and it's making them go maybe just a little bonkers.

If you are here, if you are reading this, then it's rather likely that you care about what is going on with the kids in your life, and you want to help them and maybe in the process understand what is going on inside them. The fact that you have showed up for this—picked up this book and opened it—means you have one of the most important traits a human being can possess: the desire for information. You want knowledge, you want practical examples, and you are willing to spend your extremely valuable time and energy to get those things.

Thus, I feel there is a very high statistical chance that you are awesome. And I'm not saying that just because you bought my book. (Okay, maybe buying my book is a little part of it.) But mainly, it's likely that you want to be even more awesome than you already are and are willing to do what it takes to get there. That means you have my vote right away.

All Right, but Who Am I?

So why on earth should you care that I think you are awesome, other that the fact that it shows how extremely smart and insightful I am? And why is someone with no letters to speak of after her name writing a book about such a complicated neurological issue?

My name is Jennifer, and I have Sensory Processing Disorder, which in my case comes along with a large side order of Asperger's Syndrome.

When I got diagnosed with Asperger's, it led me to a book or three about SPD, which changed my life drastically for the better. It turns out that learning about SPD is a valuable and powerful venture, even if you are in your 30s when it happens.

Yes, I got my diagnosis as an adult. It was in 2002, in fact, when I was 36. (Please take a moment to flip to the photo of me on the back cover, so you can immediately e-mail or Facebook me and tell me I look much too young to have been 36 in 2002. It's the polite thing to do.)

While I had no official diagnosis as a kid, everybody knew that "something's the matter with Jennifer." There were teachers who threw up their hands regularly and a few who regarded me as basically a problem with feet.

3

Something weird was going on—I just didn't get the information I was supposed to be getting or understand the super-obvious things that any child my age could understand. My assessment test scores and classroom performance didn't line up, and my behavior often challenged, confused, and annoyed teachers who believed "she's bright enough to know better."

But why does all this matter? Well, first of all, I'm obviously fascinating … okay, maybe I'm not *intrinsically* the most fascinating person in the world—maybe not even in the top 10, or 1,000,000. BUT. I did go through a childhood pattern that will be extremely familiar to a whole lot of parents and teachers, and, now that I'm grownup, I'm able to explain what it's like on the inside of SPD.

I also grew up with parents who had no idea of what "Sensory Processing Disorder" might be (it was the olden days, remember?), yet I was lucky enough to have a mother who was more than sharp enough to be able to tell that something was going on. In fact, all three of her kids grew up with different forms of SPD, and she rose to the challenge by reading about child development and developing her own ways to get us going and keep us functional. She's a pretty good mom.

That means I have a lot of tips, tricks, and examples for you about facing SPD in childhood and overcoming it. These include interventions (my mom being clever) that are now standard recommendations and problems I encountered needlessly that you might be able to avoid. I also have a background of classroom issues that I will share in gory detail.

Being diagnosed as an adult meant having a chance to really understand and wrestle with my own SPD. I've found a ton of ways to modify situations and my responses to them, and I've been able to genuinely change and improve my sensory processing abilities in several different ways. The stories about my life post-diagnosis are about getting better and doing better.

But while I do have SPD and am up to my earlobes in anecdotes and ideas, that doesn't mean you're going to just get my own personal story and nothing else. I've done a lot more research than just living with SPD and with other people who have it.

Once I was diagnosed with Asperger's, I found information on SPD pretty quickly. Not only did I start reading everything I could about it, I started asking people questions. I spoke with lots of people, asked lots of questions, and gleaned lots and lots of useful input.

I attended autism conferences, sensory conferences, special-needs conferences, education conferences—anything I could get to where I could possibly learn more. That means I've met lots of parents, teachers, psychologists, occupational therapists, speech therapists—all kinds of people interested in helping kids live and learn better.

It turns out that if you ask anyone and everyone to make an appointment to talk for just a little bit in person or by phone, a lot of people will give you 20 or 30 minutes of their time. I've interviewed a lot of people about their experiences with SPD and kids. I try to make sure I don't take too much time, and I always politely take "no" for an answer—it's never an advantage to be a time suck or annoyance.

It's been a wonderful mix of newbies, old hands, and genuine experts. I've interviewed parents whose child just got diagnosed with SPD, and I've spoken with OTs with years or decades of practice in helping kids overcome SPD. Even a few nationally or internationally renowned experts have found a few minutes to answer a question or two for me.

I've had great luck. Eventually I managed to work my way into speaking gigs at conferences, which means meeting more speakers. Carol Kranowitz has told me some great stories. She rocks! Temple Grandin has taught me a great deal about SPD, autism, and how genetic problems can affect the process of moving hogs from one place to another. She rocks as well!

Then there are the books, articles, and digging in to the existing research. I've read everything from the writings of parents who described their own personal journeys to pieces I found in professional peer-reviewed journals. Sometimes I read stuff so technical that I have to send out a bunch of e-mails just to find someone who can explain it on my level. Sometimes I read stuff that is just plain fun and funny. And sometimes parents break my heart with their personal stories of trying to help their children just be able to eat, sleep, or play like other kids.

If you are a parent, teacher, or anyone who works with kids on a regular basis, I do have one advantage over you: I have time to do this. My life has turned into a whirlwind of reading and interviews and speaking and writing. And that's what I can bring to you.

The reason I'm telling you all of this is to let you know that I've made every effort to get good information to help you. If I tell a story about my childhood, there's a darn good chance it's supported by research and experiences from a number of sources. Sure, I love talking about myself, and I personally find myself pretty fascinating, but the stories here are chosen to sync up with what really works for real kids.

You deserve good information, and the stories and ideas herein have been carefully chosen to represent the best knowledge I can find on SPD. Please keep that in mind when I tell you that my third-grade teacher was sometimes a total stinky poop-head.

Having awesome parents and lots of opportunities for helpful activities made my childhood better than it would have been without intervention. Learning about SPD as an adult has given me the ability to live life more fully and joyfully. That's something I want to share with you.

Chapter 2

I, Me, Mine

With or without a diagnosis, Sensory Processing Disorder (SPD) can play out in many different ways. There is no one-size-fits-all diagnosis, because SPD can affect every single sense, any one sense, or any combination of senses. There are kids who are dangerously impervious to pain; there are also kids who are so sensitive they can barely tolerate normal interactions with things like clothes and furniture.

Here's how it played out for me.

As a child, I was one of those "underachiever" kids whose report cards always had comments like "Jennifer won't apply herself to the material" and "Does not work up to expectations."

Of course, I underwent testing to see what was wrong with me. Like a lot of (ahem) underachievers, I wound up getting a cluster of diagnoses that fit me badly, if at all, and didn't help one bit.

Let's see—there was the Freudian who diagnosed me with a father fixation. I also got diagnosed with bipolar I disorder and bipolar II disorder, even though my moods, activities, and actual life contradicted those labels pretty severely. Then again, my actual life, behavior, and emotions did not equate to attention-deficit disorder (ADD), attention-deficit/hyperactivity disorder (ADHD), or a very vaguely explained label of "learning disabled."

7

It was frustrating. I had problems, real problems, but when I tried to talk about them, no one believed me. If I said that the noise in the classroom was too confusing and distracting for me to be able to do the self-paced science modules, I was told that since the other children were all working nicely and having no problems at all, obviously I was just making excuses to goof off.

There were all kinds of problems I couldn't explain, like my inability to focus any attention on the teacher if I sat behind other children to the internal feeling of chaos and detachment that hit me like a lead pipe when my teachers decided we would learn to work in groups better if all of our desks were arranged in clusters rather than rows.

These weren't minor problems; there were months on end when I was white-knuckling through my entire school day, unable to explain that I was in pain and unable even to identify exactly what that pain involved.

You've no doubt heard or experienced the same kinds of stories if you have (or were, or are) the kind of kid who is completely distracted by sounds that no one else notices or is overwhelmed by colorful classrooms that are set up to encourage groups of kids to interact throughout the day.

Eventually, I learned that no one was going to "get" my complaints about how impossible it was for me to function in a typical classroom. By then, I was in junior high, so pretty much all of the students I knew were pretty miserable at school. Hey, if grades 7-10 agree with you, you're probably a space alien or a mutant (not that there's anything wrong with that).

I struggled mightily with school, felt drained and mentally fried at the end of just about every school day, and couldn't find anyone who could figure out what was wrong with me, or with my life, or with what was going on in general.

It was frustrating. Later, I was repeatedly diagnosed with severe clinical depression, which is kind of like going to the doctor and getting a diagnosis of "you don't feel well." I already knew I was depressed—but why? Where was all this coming from? What was going on?

I was pretty darn sure something weird was going on in my brain, and nobody seemed to be able to identify it. Eventually I got tired of trying to get help, and I just plain stopped trying.

Fast-forward a few years. Okay, fast-forward a lot of years. My younger brother, 24 years my junior, was diagnosed with autism at the age of 4. Not long after that, a pattern started in my conversations with my mom. The basic structure of the statements she would casually make was something along the lines of, "They say he does X because he has autism, but you did X more than he does."

"They say he spins a lot because he has autism, but you did a lot more spinning."

"They say he recites TV shows because he has autism, but you did it even more, and we didn't even have a VCR back then."

"They say he's fussy about food because he has autism, but you were just as fussy."

And so on. And on, and on, and on.

I didn't actually think much of this pattern until I found myself more and more frustrated while trying to finish my bachelor's degree. Attempting to process data (a lecture) while in a small room with 30 other students when the whiteboard markers always seemed to be the "extra pungent all the time" brand was grueling work that left me physically exhausted. I stuck with it and got my degree (applause here), but the frustrations and setbacks I experienced told me something more was going on than typical college life.

My husband Gary (whom you will be hearing more about later) pointed out that I'd been diagnosed as "learning disabled" when I was younger, and he thought that maybe looking into that might help. Even if it wasn't a correct diagnosis, it was a starting point.

So, I started poking around. Libraries and the Internet provided me with information about this thing called "Asperger's Syndrome" and how it was related to autism.

(Yes, I know I'm talking about the autism stuff a lot—don't panic, I will get to the SPD stuff soon and stay on it for a long time.)

After some serious Googling, I tracked down a local psychologist who specialized in ADHD, learning disabilities, and autism spectrum disorders. I wanted someone who would understand and be able to clearly tell the difference between these often-confusing diagnoses.

Towards the end of my first session, I asked if he thought I had Asperger's. He replied that I was the most Aspergian person he'd ever met, and my childhood behaviors and activities were not just consistent with Asperger's— but almost a definition of it.

I was delighted, thrilled, and freaked out. I had looked for so long for some kind of reason or structure for this specific set of problems, and Asperger's clearly fit me. More importantly, a diagnosis of Asperger's meant the chance to gather the data I needed to improve myself, my social functioning, and my life in general. With the ability to get at precisely what was happening came the power to do all that good "Serenity Prayer" stuff—find out what I could and couldn't fix, find out what didn't need fixing anyway, and generally have a grasp on what the heck was going on.

And for the first 2 weeks after my diagnosis, I cried every night. Suddenly, all the years of thinking that if I just tried a little bit harder, everything would snap into place were ended, and I mourned that belief. Realizing that I would never be some of the things I thought I would be able to be was painful. No matter how good my self-esteem or self-image was, this was a radical shift and it hit me hard emotionally.

One of the first books I picked up after my diagnosis was called *Asperger Syndrome* and *Sensory Issues*. It's a book designed for use by teachers and other people who like tables, charts, and checklists. It's oriented toward adults who were dealing with grade-school children's sensory problems in the classroom. It's absolutely not the first book I would advise an adult with SPD to read.

It blew my mind and changed my life forever.

Oh, there are better first books on SPD, but that didn't matter. What mattered was that someone had put down on paper the idea that not everyone experiences sensory input the same way.

Now, that last bit seems obvious. If we all experienced sensory input the same way, we'd all prefer to listen to the same music, wear the same styles, and eat the same foods pretty much all of the time.

But it had never occurred to me that the way other people experienced the world might be significantly different than mine, in ways that greatly changed their emotional and practical reactions to things like shopping, eating out, going to the park, and just plain being.

All of a sudden it became blatantly obvious that the people who inhabited my world were probably not as mean, difficult, or casually cruel as they seemed to be. Their reactions to life weren't nearly as bizarre as they had seemed before, and their inability to understand me when I tried to explain serious problems was no longer stone headed or mean spirited. They were doing the best they could with the information they had, and so was I. We just didn't have all the data.

While I'm going to go into some really solid detail on what SPD is in the next chapter, I'll give you a little rundown of a few of my own SPD issues here. I tend to have a hypersensitive sense of smell, poor audio filtering, and difficulty hearing nonverbal speech sounds (like the sounds of the letters "T" and "P").

Then there's the fight-or-flight reflex thing: Like a lot of people with SPD, my tactile and visual responses are set up so I get into that all-out fight-or-flight, adrenaline-addled, ready-to-rip-out-a-tiger's-throat mental state quickly and effectively in totally inappropriate situations.

Note: I would never actually rip out a tiger's throat. The big cats of the wild are gorgeous creatures, and I would never do anything that might diminish the number of cute animal videos being added to YouTube. OMG, did you see the one where the tigers and lions in that zoo got big cardboard boxes to play with? Go watch it—I'll wait.

See, your sensory apparatus and the parts of your brain that are in charge of basic survival instincts are hooked up in ways that are not always ideal for modern life. These wonky hookups are even more problematic for those of us with sensory disorders.

For example, you and I both have a natural startle reflex that responds to unexpected touch. This means that when someone unexpectedly bumps into you or taps you on the shoulder, you start a bit and possibly feel a little tense until you see that it's not actually a giant monster behind you.

Similarly, suddenly seeing unexpected movement will startle most people—like if someone jumps out and goes "Boo!"

For most people, these startle reflexes are no big deal—a jump, a start, and then you shrug or laugh off the mild surprise that hit you. If that much.

If the defensive systems in your brain are usually turned up to 11, you may have a different experience. SPD can in fact turn those startle instincts up to the maximum, where instead of buzzing at you from a tiny built-in computer speaker, your panic button blasts you with a virtual Marshall stack of adrenaline.

That's a lot of adrenaline. A lot.

A slight unexpected touch can create a severe panic attack. Seeing sudden movements in your peripheral vision can provoke fear, anger, and unsightly panic-sweat. It sucks, and I've got it in spades.

Reading about SPD gave me the key to dealing with those feelings. For years, people would tap me on the shoulder or walk past me while I was trying to focus on something and I'd get intensely upset. How could they possibly be such jerks as to TAP me on the SHOULDER when I was focused on something else? Surely everyone must know that an unexpected tap would set off a total freak-out that I was now stuck trying to process instead of whatever I had been planning on doing for the next hour.

But everyone didn't know this. I had thought it was incredibly obvious that interrupting someone lost in thought was blatantly hostile and was clearly designed to cause, at minimum, discomfort, and at worst, outright pain from the overwhelming sensation of panic.

So, now I knew something important about other people: They had no way of knowing how inconveniently sensitive my senses could be and they had no way of realizing that they might be causing me serious distress by interrupting me, popping out suddenly, tapping me on the shoulder, walking on the edges of my peripheral vision, or doing any of the typical everyday actions that I found truly awful. They were not being cavalier about my feelings, much less hostile. They were just doing stuff.

As great as it was to understand that the world was not nearly as hostile and heartless as it had seemed, it led to something much bigger, much more important, and much more empowering.

Yes, I said empowering. I try to avoid nonsense words, but in this case it's the right word. The vital information I got from learning about SPD gave me real power over my own life. It provided a basic tool for me to learn to be more emotionally resilient and generally functional.

The second key thing I learned when I started reading everything I could find on SPD was that my brain was not always an accurate source of information. In fact, no human brain really is.

When someone startled me and I had a panic attack, my brain was telling me that something really, really bad had happened, and *it was wrong*. The level of what had happened was actually "mild inconvenience" or "somewhat annoying," not "THE WORLD IS CRASHING DOWN AROUND ME!!!!!!"

Neither I nor you nor anyone else can get to the point where the instinctive, neurologically based feelings of anger, fear, anxiety, and other counterproductive responses to input can be totally prevented or simply brushed aside with no effort. Those feelings may not be factually accurate, but they are real, and they are powerful.

When you're in that fight-or-flight state, you lose the ability to take in new information—you are so focused on possible threats that you are not up for a rational discussion of why the adrenaline coursing through your body is merely a biochemical response that does not necessarily accurately reflect the actual needs of the situation.

Nope, when you get that burst of adrenaline, you freak out. Especially if you are 6 years old and in a tense or difficult situation. Even mature adults don't tend to be mellow and friendly once that trigger is activated.

There is a difference between how a parent reacts when a child asks to go to the bathroom in a mellow moment at home and how that same parent reacts to that same child when they are at the mall 2 days before Christmas and they have at least 10 presents they have to find before dinnertime. Stress makes behaving sanely difficult.

And yet knowing, really knowing, that at least some of the anger and anxiety I felt was based on improperly processed data helped me a lot. It meant I didn't have to fix everything all the time. I didn't have to make sure that person who interrupted me rudely never did it again by making them understand very clearly exactly how painful and upsetting their actions were—which is, of course, something that can only be accomplished with prolonged yelling, lecturing, general freaking out, and other exhausting procedures.

Knowing that the rougher parts of my brain didn't get to rule me—that I didn't have to be the servant of every moment of panic or pain—was a major breakthrough that has helped me massively.

But.

There's always a "but."

Let me tell you a story. It's about one amazing set of events that made me understand how important understanding SPD was to me personally.

THE MALL

When I was a teenager I read an article that explained how important the mall was to our economy and society. The mall is to modern American what the town square and general store once were: a place where communities developed connection. It forms a social and commercial hub that has major sociological significance, and is vital.

I mentioned the Asperger's thing. Those of us who are Aspies are often big readers, and we tend to be very rule bound. That article on the meaning and significance of THE MALL in modern life hit me quite hard. It clearly meant that my difficulty with making social connections was at least partially caused by spending too little time at the mall.

So, in my late 20s, I developed the habit of going to the mall every Saturday morning. I saved up errands. If I needed a birthday card for someone, needed my shoes repaired, or had to get some new socks, then I put that on the agenda for my weekly mall trip.

And it was tough. The mall is a very loud and crowded place by 11 AM on Saturday. Every store has its own background music, as does the mall itself, and they seldom blend well. Visuals such as storefronts and merchandise displays are carefully set up to grab your attention, generating a constant interplay of conflicting bits of gaudy eye candy and sparse but striking visuals that overwhelms the brain.

The smells are intense, too. Not only is there the food court, but there are perfumes and makeup for sale, which means oodles of scents fighting each other. Dashing through a department store to get past the dreaded sprayers and the people who want to put the latest foundation on you is like running the gauntlet. And some stores just outright pump scent into their own space and even out into the mall proper to get your attention and put you in the mood to buy.

I will not discuss Cinnabon here.

Sounds, sights, smells—even without crowds, malls are torturous. There often are crowds, people moving around in unpredictable ways, none of them keeping pace with each other, all talking, laughing, shopping, sweating, and otherwise producing unbelievable amounts of sensory noise.

Then there is the worst of all creatures, the person who walks just barely almost inside my peripheral vision. Since they walk at a slightly different pace than me and at a variable pace, their arms and body dart in and out of my field of vision so I am constantly jumpy, always aware that there is something there, following me, not quite visible but definitely palpable, like a predator stalking its prey.

Little kids run around at random. They are smelly and make noise. Somehow they give the impression of stickiness even without touching me.

I went to the mall *every Saturday* for years, until I read about SPD. It then struck me that maybe the mall was not the ideal milieu for my personal shopping needs.

It had never occurred to me that the other people at the mall didn't understand that they were constantly startling and stalking me. I had always taken my stress and panic at the mall as signs that I was a wussy and that I needed to toughen up and get with the program.

With this new knowledge, I decided that if I was going to have to be "tough" sometimes because of my SPD, I would pick those times more carefully. The "buy one get one at 50% off" sale at Hot Topic was just not worth it.

I stopped going to the mall. I started having much more pleasant and relaxing weekends. It wasn't until weeks later that my husband mentioned a very, very, very important thing.

We had not had a single fight on a weekend since I had stopped going to the mall.

I had it up TO HERE with my husband many times on weekends. Lotsa big fights over little things, but I knew there had to be something more to it.

I'd read enough pop psychology and women's magazines to know that if I were getting that angry over the little things that happened on the weekends, it was a sign of a more serious underlying problem. I was determined to get at that problem and excise it from my marriage, like the cancerous tumor it was.

And then I stopped getting angry on weekends, not through undergoing weeks of therapy or via some massive psycho-emotional breakthrough—but simply because I stopped going to the mall.

Oh, I looked for other possible reasons, but all of our usual weekend interactions were just as they'd always been. Gary continued to do chores differently than I do them, which meant he was doing them wrong, but I just didn't mind that so much. I could live with a few dusty spots, no biggie.

Seriously, no biggie. All of a sudden, the little things that bothered me were so very much smaller. I didn't need to correct things. I didn't feel disrespected or like my feelings didn't matter to him. (I know my feelings matter to him because he bought me Thor and Loki bobble heads, for heaven's sake.)

It became possible for me to just let a lot of stuff slide, and it was also possible for me to complain in a friendly way sort of way when something wasn't at the slide-worthy level. My husband hadn't changed, the marriage hadn't changed, but the big fights had stopped.

Without that weekly trip to the mall filling me with adrenaline, panic, and dread, I was no longer primed to blow. Oh, we disagreed and argued sometimes, but it was nothing dramatic.

Without a morning full of pain and adrenaline, I changed over from getting enraged to getting annoyed—and often to just letting some things go.

It's pretty simple, really: Pain makes anger happen. Eliminating a source of completely unnecessary pain is a great way to cut back on anger.

Once my husband pointed out the salutary effects of avoiding the mall, I made sure I continued to avoid it to the greatest extent possible. If I had to shop in the brick-and-mortar world, I went to detached stores, or, if the mall was the best place to get something, I would do surgical-strike shopping: Pick a specific target, get in, grab the goods, get out, and never look back.

Hard Work and Hard Head

In the years since I first started learning about SPD, I've done a LOT of things to help mitigate my sensory problems and improve my reactions to potentially dicey sensory input. I've done a lot of walking, indoors and out, to soothe my anxiety; I've improved my sensory diet; and I've generally worked hard to feed my head lots of nourishing input.

I've spent years digging up a whole lot of information on what they call "cognitive behavioral therapy" and the related cognitive therapies, which are amazingly helpful when dealing with the anxiety, anger, and stress that can come along with SPD.

In fact, I've changed my brain a lot. It used to be that what seemed like minor scrapes and bruises to others sent me into a tailspin of pain and fear. After years of learning to process the emotional part of pain, I respond to pain in general about a thousand times more calmly. Except if I stub my toe. Stubbed toes are awful and should be outlawed.

I'm going to cover what I've done and what you and your child can learn to do, based on actual science (Thomas Dolby music sting here), because I've road tested so much of it that I have learned to take something that designed for more general purposes, like cognitive behavioral therapy, and apply it to the specific situations a person with SPD winds up in.

I've come a long way. A loooooong way. I've done a lot of learning and made a lot of mistakes, and I hope to spare you some of the time and energy of that process by boiling it down to the most useful bits.

But no matter where you are when it comes to dealing with your own and/or your child's and/or your student's SPD, there's one thing you should know: Perfect isn't possible or necessary. You don't have to know everything, you don't have to avoid mistakes, and you don't have to make all of the problems go away forever to make your child's life better now.

This past December, I wanted to find a particular calendar and realized that my best bet was the seasonal calendar place at the mall. You know, that kiosk that pops up at every mall sometime in November and disappears at the start of January, and sells nothing but lots and lots of different calendars.

So, a visit to the mall in December was in order. And I had a bum ankle, which meant I could only get around slowly and painfully by using a crutch and a "walking boot."

I went to the mall, and I found that (*a*) the crowds for the Christmas season started earlier than I thought and (*b*) the calendar kiosk no longer existed at this particular mall. At all.

Simply learning that involved the usual issue of fighting my way through zillions of people, many of them teens performing that weird dance of shopping/socializing/being hormone addled that makes us all love puberty so much. In other words, there was lots of chaos, lots of people whose movement patterns made no sense, and a ton of noise and smells and WHY DO THEY ALWAYS PUT HOT DOG ON A STICK RIGHT NEXT TO CINNABON???? ARE THEY TRYING TO MAKE ME CRAZY????

I got through it. I got in, got out, and got gone as quickly as reasonably possible. I even found one thing I'd been looking everywhere for, just by random chance. Yay.

But after I got home, my husband did something that really bugged me, and instead of blowing it off like I always do, I started a fight. A big, nasty fight.

Oh, it was much shorter and quieter than in the bad old days. And, neither of us got as upset or as overwhelmed as back then.

I've done things right. I've learned to change, overcome, and deal with my SPD incredibly well. And, yet, sometimes it just doesn't work. Sometimes the sensory panic monster attacks, and I react/overreact in ways I'm not thrilled with.

The only path to success is through roughly five zillion failures, and the only way to stop having bad patches is to give up and stop growing. You can't protect anyone, not even yourself, from everything.

Incidentally, it didn't take either me or my husband all that long to figure out what was going on and to disarm. We've got mad skills now.

You can have mad skills, too. Read on.

Understanding Sensory Processing Differences

While it is important to discuss how each sense can be affected by SPD, and explain what the different kinds of SPD are, first I want to cover a bit about how the brain's sophisticated sensory processing affects your everyday life, and talk a bit about how your brain is constantly parsing, filtering, and prioritizing your sensory input for you without you having to even be aware of it.

Everyone reading this has sensory organs that allow them to take in data. Some of you might have one or another that is less perfect (or even nonfunctional), but we all have sensory organs and systems.

The problem lies in the fact that working sensory organs and functional sensory processing are two different things. There are a ton of factors, many of them not well understood, that affect whether a given sensory input is ever even noticeable to us.

Doctors and researchers have known for a looooong time that occurrences like concussions and strokes can have a major effect on how people see the world around them. People who have no damage to their sensory organs can have profound changes in what they see, hear, and otherwise sense in the world around them after experiencing physical trauma to the brain, whether it's major or minor. And that's not counting the day-to-day differences individuals experience.

Two people who both have 20/20 vision can have very different abilities when it comes to seeing what's there. One may notice instantly when something in his visual environment changes, while another may fail to notice for months before saying, "When did that Red Lobster become a drugstore? And wasn't it something else in between?"

So perfect eyesight doesn't guarantee that a person will understand or remember visual information very well. And it doesn't guarantee having a "sense" of color or distance. One person can easily tell what looks good as far as clothing, haircuts, or room decor go, while another always looks like he or she chooses all of the above completely at random.

The same thing applies to hearing: Some people have an excellent sense of pitch, while others who perform just as well on hearing tests are tone-deaf. Turns out that just because you can hear the full range of humanly detectable pitches does not mean you can make any sense of them.

There are people with the ability to smell and taste every little detail of perfumes or wines, and some of those people are able to make good livings working as professional "noses." (Of course, there are also people who fool themselves into thinking they have the ability to distinguish "vanilla notes with hints of cinnamon and wet dog" in a wine, but that's another issue altogether.)

And we all know that some people are more startled by unexpected touch than others. Some people go through a "haunted house" attraction laughing most of the time, while others experience even the most mild and hackneyed amateur haunting as if it were a genuinely threatening situation (I fall into the latter category).

Heck, the ordinary senses of where our bodies are and how we are moving are vastly different from person to person. Babies are born without a clear idea of where they stop and where the world begins. All that cute sticking their feet into their mouths is a vital part of locating their bodies. Touching and mouthing gives babies tons of information about what they are seeing, so that eventually they can tell a lot about the shape of an object just by looking at it.

Most people probably don't notice that when a baby's chewing on stuff, playing with its own feet, clapping its hands, or grasping everything in reach, it's actually developing the ability to process what it's seeing and hearing. Just being born with eyes and ears that work doesn't cut it. There's a ton of work to be done just to have a shot at using your eyes to coordinate what you're doing with your hands. It's completely nuts.

Is it any wonder that this super-complex process of making heads or tails out of what we sense can be less than ideal for some people? Despite the huge range of what constitutes "normal" (or functional) sensory processing, some kids don't develop all the connections and knowledge they need to simply get through the day of seeing, hearing, and feeling what they need to.

In fact, it's pretty amazing that our senses and our brains work together as well as they do. We take for granted that we are going to get the input we need every day, But we all have moments when our sensory processing becomes noticeable, and when it does, we get a little insight into what SPD is.

Sensory Moments

Of course, we all have what I call "sensory moments." Those are the times when we are brought face to face with the wild and seemingly inexplicable differences between what we sense one day and the next—sometimes even one moment and the next. We all have sensory moments, and they can help us understand SPD better.

For most people, sensory moments demonstrate the elegance and functionality of well-tuned sensory processing. And, they tell us something about what's missing when a kid has SPD.

If you drive a car, you may have noticed that some mornings you get into your car, start it up, and the radio starts blaring at an utterly intolerable level. When you got out of the car the night before, the music sounded great, but when you start up the car in the morning, it's unbelievably LOUD, so loud you couldn't tolerate it for one more second! You were having a great time cranking it last time you were in the car, but now you turn it off as fast as you can.

This is because your hearing automatically adjusts to the sounds around you without you even noticing it. Your brain knows it has to hear things other than the radio (or the chatter in your office, or the shuffle of 30 kids taking notes), so it tunes out the sounds that are unimportant. After all, if you're driving, the radio is not nearly as important to your well-being as your ability to hear squealing brakes ahead of you or an ambulance siren behind.

So the brain tunes out constant, non-vital sounds—that is, those sounds that don't actually require your attention. Every time you hear a song you love on the radio, you consciously want to hear it better, so you turn it up. You don't necessarily turn it down when the song is over, so your brain gradually starts to ignore the less-interesting constant blare from the radio. Your brain can do this over and over, without you even noticing it.

That sound you hear when you start up your car in the morning—that horrific blast of sound coming out of nowhere—tells you that your brain is capable of doing some fancy sensory processing that allows you to tune out what amounts to background noise. If you didn't have that sound-filtering ability, you'd hear lots of noises that would interfere with your thinking and functioning. You'd hear the noise of the engine, the sound of the radio, the heating or air conditioning, and all the little sounds of the road equally, and you'd be overwhelmed by the constant noise. If someone tried to talk to you when all these sounds were pressing into your consciousness, you wouldn't be able to make out a word they said.

That's what happens to children with poor audio processing. The difference is that if you have lousy audio processing, you might be able to filter in some circumstances and not in others, but without any predictability. That child may hear the sound of other children doing worksheets in the classroom at an intense level, because the brain doesn't know what to tune out and what to tune in.

In your car, you can turn the radio up or down to suit you. If your passenger wants to talk, you can just turn a knob or push a button and be fine. The kid with poor audio filtering can't just turn down the sounds that distract him. He's stuck spending time every single day confused by the muddle of input he's getting.

When you get in your car in the morning, you are the same person you were last night, with the same ears and the same brain as you were last night. The exact same input feels really, really, really different to you—the loudness goes from awesome to awful literally overnight.

This is true for kids with lousy audio processing, too. There are kids who can focus on the teacher's voice just fine first thing the morning, when they are freshly rested and fed, but they lose that filtering ability as the day wears on. There are other kids who can't "wake up" their brains well enough to make sense of sound until they get some physical activity to awaken their brains and get those filters up and running. Both kinds of children will be able to respond appropriately to their teacher sometimes and be truly unable to do so at other times. This is the kind of problem that can make kids seriously cranky and frustrated, while driving their teachers to invest in the mega-jumbo bottle of ibuprofen.

Your Name Here

Another sensory moment many people have experienced is called "cocktail party hearing." That term is old, dating back to the real days of *Mad Men*, when normal, middle-class human beings actually had such parties.

Cocktail-party hearing is the near-universal experience of being in a room with many people conversing (apparently over martinis while nibbling on small things wrapped in other things), and while you converse with your neighbor, you are pretty much oblivious to other conversations. All you hear is your own conversation and a vague murmur from the rest of the room.

And that lasts right up until the moment someone says your name. You couldn't have said what any one conversation in that room was about, but then someone in one of those conversations mentions you, and you hear your name loud and clear. Your attention instantly switches focus to locate the source of the sound and hone in on what is being said about you.

It's a rather amazing thing. It's another example of the elegance of typical sensory processing. You don't have to be aware of who is talking to whom or what anyone is saying up to that very second. Your brain is doing its bit to help you function in that situation: It's filtering out all those other people so you can focus on whatever mid-60s-style business deal you are trying to close. But some part of your nervous system, something in your brain, is still listening just enough that the mere mention of your own name immediately and completely shifts your focus. It's like magic.

Going from oblivious to razor-sharp in half a second is an amazing example of how involved sensory processing is. If your ears are working fine, you'd think you would hear what is nearest to you best, but that's not how the brain works. The brain has layers of awesomeness designed to protect and aid you socially so you can function as a member of a species in which individuals need social connectedness just to survive. It isn't as though there is any threat to your physical well-being here, but you do need to be alert to how others see you (and whether they are volunteering you as a chaperone for the school camping trip). And your brain just casually does that for you.

Is it any wonder that a delicate and amazingly specific bit of sensory processing like this can go awry? When the brain struggles just to filter out enough of the noise in the room to make sense of what's going on, how on earth can the nervous system find the energy to keep you socially aware and alert? It's no wonder that kids with SPD have social difficulties—they may not even notice if something they've done is causing the other kids consternation, because all of the lovely filtering that would alert them to being talked about ain't gonna happen. Man. It sucks when your sensory processing isn't all it needs to be.

So, What Is Sensory Processing Disorder?

Good question. There are a lot of unanswered questions out there about how our brains actually do sensory processing and what it means when someone's brain can't do it right. If someone tells you they know exactly how to locate sensory processing problems in the brain and in what parts of the brain the specific problems lie, they are mistaken. Okay, there might be some people on the cutting edge of neurological research who have some pretty darn good theories, but the anatomy and biochemistry and other stuff that may make up SPD has not yet been mapped out.

We still do know something about what SPD is. SPD happens when a person's brain does not make good enough sense of sensory input for that person to complete the tasks of daily life without serious impediments. This means tasks like learning, playing, eating, moving, and working become way harder than they should be. A person with SPD is getting inaccurate, muddled, or inconsistent information so often that they consistently can't behave or perform up to reasonable expectations for someone of that person's age, education, and experience.

Okay, let me break that down a little. I said "can't" behave, which is important. A kid whose brain refuses to do the filtering necessary to tune out unimportant noises or the cocktail-party hearing thing happen often can't pay good attention to verbal directions.

Every kid (and every adult) has times when she just won't do what she's told for any of a zillion reasons. Every kid and adult has times when they are too flaked out from lack of sleep or other physical problems to follow directions well.

But when a child whose hearing test results are just fine consistently can't make sense of verbal directions, then there may be something else going on.

This is important. It is pretty likely that in a given classroom of, say, 32 students, there are 32 somewhat different experiences of each activity, lesson, and stimulus. One child always wants to color in red, because red is the best color ever, while another wants blue, blue, blue everything. One kid is great at drawing, while another excels in reading, and yet another is great at any kind of physical activity. Different interests, different talents, that's pretty much par for the course.

In SPD, the differences are much more extreme. Kids with SPD may be super-sensitive or super-insensitive to any given kind of sensory input, and one kid may have very different sensitivity levels when different kinds of input are involved.

What's interesting, important, and something else that begins with "i" is that it is possible for a person like me to have an extremely varied and problematic sense of what is going on around them and even within them. This can result in all kinds of problem behaviors which no amount of discussion or scolding can change.

It can look like immaturity or acting out—or like depression, or confusion. Age-appropriate behavior can be far out of reach when a kid has SPD.

We all know there is an age at which is it hard for a really little kid to grasp a small paper cup with just that right degree of firmness so that they don't drop it or crush it. As most kids develop, they get a better sense of the amount of pressure they need to use, the weight of the cup, and how their fingers and hand coordinate to hold things.

We may think an older child who constantly falls is hopelessly clumsy or "off in the clouds," but we rightly expect that babies and toddlers will fall down a lot, even when sitting right on the floor. A baby who can sit up can easily lean over too far when trying to grasp a nearby object. The result is an adorable YouTube video of a kid who goes to pet the doggie and can't rebalance fast enough to stay upright when the doggie moves. The startled look on a baby's face when she realizes that gravity is no respecter of persons is mind-bendingly cute.

In most cases, as kids develop, they naturally learn to sit upright without tipping or sliding out of places, to hold a wide variety of objects with the correct grip, to stand and walk and run with confidence, and to respond quickly to changes in their surroundings, such as a dog who decides that enough is enough.

We accept crushing and dropping things, tripping or leaning and falling, and generally failing as a natural part of childhood development. But not every child's brain can learn to coordinate these things at the same rate, nor with the same amount of success. The simple ability to respond to his surroundings appropriately can elude a child with SPD for far longer than average.

All of the senses, all of the systems that allow us to know where we are, what is going on around us, and how we can interact with our surroundings are super-mega-ultra dependent on having the right kind of processing develop in the brain.

SPD is the result of the fact that not all brains automatically learn to do what is needed for a kid to function as a kid.

There has been great research over the past few decades on what exactly kids with SPD are missing, what drives their behaviors, and what to do about it. There is also a whole lot of lingo describing what is happening when that kid can't successfully walk across the room while holding a cup of liquid or filter sounds well enough to be able to follow directions. The words are important enough to explain and problematic enough to explain even more than that. Let's begin.

SPD, Sensory Issues & Sensory Differences

There is some serious confusion about the terminology related to SPD. Alas, I cannot clear up all of the problems with this book, but I am going to explain what the terminology means and how I understand it and use it. Words are, for an awful lot of us, a big part of the thinking process, so I hope to help you think about SPD in a relatively coherent way by working through the words.

First, a recap: Sensory Processing Disorder, or SPD, means that a person has one or more senses that are processed badly or oddly by the brain to the extent that it interferes with normal activities, development, learning, and social functioning. A child with super-slow response times to audio input my take a minute or two longer to open his book than the other kids do, which means he's always running behind and missing some of the lesson. If an adult is so sensitive to unexpected touch that she freaks out when she is tapped on the arm, that will interfere with her social functioning.

The term SPD always refers to something that causes problems. A person with SPD will need some kind of assistance or coping mechanism to be able to get things done. This can come from parents and therapists (for a child or teen) or from their own impetus (for an adult). If a person has SPD, then some kind of intervention is needed for that person to achieve their own goals, whether they want to simply kick a ball in a relatively straight-ish line or be able to behave appropriately during a job interview.

But, I'm going to use other language too. The terms *sensory issues* and *sensory differences* are going to come up a lot. Some authors have used the term *sensory issues* to mean SPD, but I think it's a bigger term than that.

Sensory issues and sensory differences are any kind of significantly atypical, non-normal ways of processing sensory input. This includes all of the stuff that comes under the heading of SPD and also stuff that is really important but not necessarily disordered.

Sensory issues can even include things like having a superior sense of pitch in music. A really good sense of pitch is pretty obviously not an SPD thing, but it is different and significant. A kid who has a superior sense of pitch and also has an overly intense fight-or-flight instinct may panic or freak out when he hears cacophonous sounds, but the solution is not to "dumb down" his sense of pitch, but to help him develop coping mechanism and ways to calm down and respond better.

I have a sensory issue that I don't consider a disorder: I am super-sensitive to certain high pitches. This has saved the scruff of a few abandoned kittens who were crying for their mothers. (In fact, I suspect that animals can sense the fact that I'm a total sucker for someone who is cute, furry, and hungry and therefore they make sure to make that kind of high-pitched noise to reel me in.) It does not generally inconvenience me, though—once in a while, I can't tolerate certain high-pitched sounds, but that's hardly abnormal and isn't a big problem for me.

My husband has a sensory issue that I envy: He doesn't experience pain nearly as intensely as most people do, but he does experience pain well enough (and fast enough) that he doesn't endanger himself. When he had gum surgery, he was warned that it would hurt for some days, but he actually didn't need any painkillers to be comfortable. At the same time, if he accidentally touches a hot skillet, he pulls his hand away instantly, just as most of us do. That means he has a strong enough sense of pain to be safe but weak enough to he avoid a lot of discomfort. It's different, but not a disorder.

Why is this so important to me? Because I think it is really important not to try to fix what isn't broken. Every child with SPD will need some kind of help, and that help should be focused on the stuff that is causing the most pain and dysfunction.

I also worry about parents who feel that their child needs to be within a normal range in the functioning and processing of every single sense. It's good to be aware of what is normal and what is healthy (not always the same thing), but it's not good to try to make a kid fit into whatever the normal range is considered to be this week.

What we consider normal changes all the time, and it varies in how useful it is, so I am taking a stand for kids who are weird but healthy. If your kid is like my husband and not all that sensitive to pain, yet is able to tell when something is too hot or cold to grasp, and to feel it when an injury requires attention, then that's good enough. And it may allow him to do things that most people can't.

Of course, if a child or adult is so super-insensitive to pain that they injure themselves and can't protect themselves against real dangers (touching a hot stove and not removing their hand fast enough to avoid a bad burn, walking on a twisted or broken ankle without getting it set), then that's a serious problem. The idea is to distinguish between "unusual" and "dire," so you can focus on your child's needs in the most effective and awesome way.

The Sensory Systems

All books on SPD are mandated by federal law and the Geneva Convention to have sections fairly close to the front that discuss the sensory systems that can be affected by SPD and what the specific forms of SPD are anyway. This means that you may have already read books with checklists of symptoms to help you determine what kind of SPD you or your child might have along with the usual explanations of the basic terminology.

I am definitely going to provide these required sections, but with a few slight changes to the usual format.

While we're in the midst of those first sections and discussing the sensory systems and SPD, I'm going to take the occasional detour to talk about my own experiences growing up with undiagnosed SPD and how getting a diagnosis affected my adult life. I'm hoping to provide a bit of insight into the difference a diagnosis makes and how these things may play out in real life.

In addition to those detours into talking about myself, I'm going to cover how I think and talk about SPD. The usual language/jargon about SPD and the sensory systems is a bit unwieldy for me personally, and I'll be talking to you about that and giving you some verbiage to make the language of SPD more accessible (I hope).

All of this information about what's what will be interspersed with stories and concrete suggestions—I'm not going to wait until the end to talk turkey. I know that it's usual to cover all of the different SPDs and all of the sensory systems before getting down to coping methods and solutions, but I'm going to go right ahead and throw a bunch of it in right off. That includes info about the inner coping processes and life skills that got me through childhood alive and how I've developed them over time.

So these coming sections aren't just about understanding and responding to SPD, but are also about the whole picture: what these things are like from the inside and what works when you are up against them.

The Eight Sensory Systems

Yes, there are EIGHT, count them, EIGHT sensory systems. Oh, yes, there are the usual five senses, but there are three more just to make it more complicated.

Actually, those three "extras" are not here to make things more complicated; rather they are things that come so naturally and easily to most people that the human race in general doesn't notice their existence. For example, one is called the "vestibular system," which is the sense that tells us exactly how gravity is pulling on us. If you're standing upright, gravity is affecting your body in a different direction than if you are hanging upside down on the jungle gym. But who thinks about stuff like that? Ever?

I'll tell you who thinks about stuff like that: many occupational therapists, quite a few knowledgeable speech pathologists, and even some primary school teachers are pretty aware that there are kids out there who don't fully get the messages their bodies are trying to send them about gravity.

Those kids may be terrified of small heights, or they may climb dangerously high, but the one thing that a fair number of kids with SPD have in common is that the pull they feel, the level of danger they sense in a possible fall, just isn't "right."

But here's the thing: Referring to the vestibular sense and the vestibular system always seems a bit confusing to me. It's not that those aren't perfectly good terms. I just need to use words that I can easily remember and understand, so I'm going to be using different terms a lot of the time. In fact, let's kick this overview of the senses off with a bit of info on the vestibular sense, also known as the …

35

Sense of Gravity

The sense of gravity, which I will sometimes call "the gravity sense" or "the gravitational sense," actually lives inside your ears. There is a little area in your inner ear, an area that is called the *vestibulum*, in which teeny little hairs respond to the movement of a very small amount of liquid that lives in there.

It's pretty amazing stuff. The inner ear is so tangled up that the part where the vestibulum is located is actually called the *labyrinth* of the inner ear. It's a labyrinth. A very small labyrinth, in fact, deep inside your ear, with a teeny part called the *vestibulum*, with tiny, tiny hairs, and it controls a huge part of how you move.

So that is where your sense of gravity comes from. Tiny hairs move around and the brain gets signals from that delicate system that tell it whether you are upright or lying down, whether you are moving or staying still.

If you're a child, the gravity sense is a big, important part of the most serious business of childhood: play. Play is how kids learn most physical and social skills, but if your sense of gravity is "off," it is pretty hard to play well with other children, or even alone.

There are kids who are undersensitive—*under-responsive* is what it's called—to gravity, so they don't really get much feedback from the world. Swinging on a swing or bouncing on a trampoline may seem pretty dull to a kid with this kind of gravity sense. In fact, he may feel "meh" about a lot of things. This includes the baby who barely responds when Mom or Dad tosses him up in the air and catches him—he's like, "Whatevs."

While the under-responsive kid is getting little feedback from his gravity sense, the overly sensitive, over-responsive kid is getting loud, crazy, urgent signals from hers. Some of the time, that was me.

When a kid's gravitational sense is keyed up too high, brisk upward or downward movement is just too much to handle. There's this thing that is called "gravitational insecurity," and it's a doozy.

Your brain has to be able to tell you when you are climbing very high and need to be careful. If you didn't have a sense of heights, you might not be aware enough of what you were doing, and then you might take heck of a tumble. It's basic, it's primal, it's a survival instinct.

That's why gravitational insecurity is a big, big deal. The kid with gravitational insecurity experiences primal terror when he climbs even a little higher than usual. He goes up the jungle gym to a height that younger children think is easy, and he balks and refuses to climb higher. He then gets called a "baby" and a "'fraidy cat," and he says something like, "Aw, this is kid stuff, I don't wanna do it anyway."

What's really going on, here? He climbs up that little bit on the jungle gym, or perhaps one or two rungs up a ladder, and in that split second when his brain gets a message from his gravity sense, he feels overwhelming gravitational insecurity. From the most primal parts of his brain, he feels absolutely terrified, as if climbing one more rung will put him in horrible, intolerable danger. So he stops.

This kid will get teased for his fear of even relatively mild heights, but ANY child who was getting the brain signals he was receiving would panic.

In fact, it is a tribute to how tough kids are, and how much these kids want to be able to play, that they keep trying time and time again.

I tried, time and time again. When I was in kindergarten, we had a separate playground from the "big kids," with a wonderful long jungle gym made to look like a dragon. I loooooved that dragon jungle gym, and I wanted desperately to climb up as high as I could go.

Day after day, I would look out at that jungle gym from the classroom and think, "Today is the day! I know I can do it, this time I will be brave!"

When I was on the ground, walking toward that dragon, I could plainly see it wasn't so very high off the ground, even at its topmost point, and that the other kids were climbing all the way up and down and having a wonderful time.

And I'd be determined to do it. I'd start at the most inviting point, all the way on the right end, and I would climb.

Some days I was very deliberate, and climbed bit by bit, slowly, figuring I could tackle it a little at a time. Some days I tried to climb as fast as I could in the hopes of getting past my fears by barreling though them.

But I stopped dead at the same spot every single time.

There was a specific height I would reach where all of a sudden the ground was very, very, very far away, and all of my body and brain cried out a warning to my very soul: This is TOO DARN HIGH! It was chilling, it was frustrating, it made no sense whatsoever to me, but it was overwhelming.

Often I would stay at that height, the last rung I could get up on before my brain started screaming, and I would try try try to find the courage to go up just one more rung. I wanted UP. I wanted to climb as high as the other kids, as high as the bravest boys, as high as I could possibly go. And I couldn't.

I wasn't scared. I was petrified. There just wasn't enough courage or strength in the world for that climb.

What was truly crazy-making was that I could clearly see the other kids climbing up ahead of me, and I knew, flat out knew, that the jungle gym wasn't very high and was perfectly safe for little children. None of that mattered, though, when I was climbing. The only thing that mattered was the truly primal fear that went screaming through my brain, that stopped me dead. Every time.

I really did prepare. For example, at that time, I went to a school where girls usually had to wear skirts, so I would wear shorts under my skirt so I could climb to any height without showing my underwear. I wanted to climb that gosh-darned dragon.

Today, I know there are OTs out there who are great with kids who have gravitational insecurity, who can gradually help a child develop a more functional gravity sense and slowly build up to climbing higher and doing more fun stuff.

If I had gravitational insecurity today, I would easily be able to do the research and work on the problem, either on my own or with an OT or another knowledgeable professional.

But darn it, at some point between kindergarten and mid-adolescence my brain shifted somehow and I wound up craving vestibular stimulation instead of shrinking from it. This resulted in a trip to Hershey Park during which I rode The Comet (the largest wooden roller coaster east of the Mississippi at the time) 19 times in one day—and spent a fair amount of time in between roller coaster rides on the giant "rocking ship" ride at the same park.

So not all problems with the gravity sense look alike, and not all differences in sensing gravity are problems. Some kids crave physical challenges to gravity, some have primal terror tied to even slight gravity challenges, and some could care less.

The difference between a sensory issue with gravity and an SPD is how much it slows down or endangers the child. As a small child with gravitational insecurity, I couldn't climb and play as well as other kids, and I felt like I was a stupid chicken, which added to my social awkwardness.

A child with a really under-responsive sense of gravity won't be terrified, but also won't have much fun on the playground. A lot of the sensory, physical, mental, and social benefits of play won't be available to her, and that sucks. It's easy to wind up as a couch potato when movement doesn't mean much to you.

A child who totally craves gravitational challenge may have SPD if they don't have the ability to avoid real danger—or if they just plain can't stay still long enough to make a friend or do a worksheet.

Remember, though, that what we are looking for is whether a child is missing out, unable to learn well, or otherwise handicapped or hampered by how well his brain detects that relationship between his inner ear and gravity. There are people, functional people, out there who avoid scary rides. There are others who love hang-gliding and bungee-jumping and those who aren't all that moved by motion yet have really good lives.

In other words, don't look to make your child normal or "easy" here. Look to make him or her more functional, able to work, play, and learn, both alone and with others. Keep that awareness that you are looking to tackle the real problems, starting with those that are truly urgent.

This holds true for every sensory system, including, of course, the muscle sense.

The Muscle Sense

The muscle sense is officially called *proprioception*, which is why I call it the *muscle sense*. The *muscle-and-joint sense* would be a more precise term, but it's a little unwieldy. The muscle sense sends information to your brain about what your muscles and joints are up to, and if you can't parse that data very well, it's a problem.

Most folks aren't even aware that they have a muscle sense. It's unusual for people to think about how they mentally calibrate how much force their muscles need to use, when a muscle can and cannot put forth some more effort, and how much bending their joints are doing at the moment. It's a completely invisible, inaudible, and very, very, very important sense.

If I ask you to lift your left arm or left leg, would you need to look at your arms or legs to pick the one to move? Probably not. But simply being able to locate and move a limb without having to consciously locate it is a very big deal for someone with an iffy muscle sense.

There are a lot of little things that require us to know what our muscles are doing. If you hold a paper cup in one hand and walk across the room, your brain has to constantly, wordlessly calculate how much pressure you are using on that cup. If you grip it too hard, you'll crush it, but if you hold it too loosely, it might slip out of your grasp. Also, you have to keep your arm bent to the correct degree so that you don't spill what's in the cup.

For someone with a less-than-ideal muscle sense, that is a seriously stressful situation. Trying to grip a paper cup just right while keeping your arm bent just right while also walking and probably being expected to be aware of your surroundings takes a whole lot of focus and determination when you aren't getting good feedback from your body.

This is a sense that takes time and work to develop in any child, but most kids go through the period where they learn all this while they are little enough that they are expected to spill things and no sane adult would actually give them, say, a cup that is almost full to the brim with juice. But if your muscle sense doesn't develop well enough in the usual allotted time, painful social and emotional events start occurring.

The kids who can't grip things to the right extent, can't keep a cup with liquid in it close enough to level, and basically lack the feedback mechanisms that make the muscle sense function better are in for some serious frustration—at minimum.

If you can't grip things with a just-right amount of pressure, having to deal with anything, anything at all, that is handed out in paper cups can be frustrating and humiliating. It doesn't matter if it's water, juice, paint, or popcorn, the second a kid realizes he has to walk from one side of the room to the other with it he has to focus with all of his might.

And after the first really spectacular spill in the classroom, other kids will often "help" by distracting the child who has the poor muscle sense. Hey, they're kids, they're rutchy, it's a half-hour until recess, and they are desperate for something to break up the morning. A big spill means they get to break out of their schedule and goof around while the teacher cleans up.

So the kid with the poor muscle sense learns quickly that anything requiring good motor skills can turn into social and emotional quicksand in seconds flat.

Think about the things kids do (and the skills they need to develop) that require excellent feedback from the joints and muscles. Heck, cutting anything at all with a pair of those blunt school scissors is almost impossible to start with. The whole process of holding the scissors, working the scissors, holding onto what they're cutting, and keeping what they're cutting in a position in which it's possible to actually cut it is pretty darn intense to start with. Add poor muscle feedback and you have a frustrating mess.

(I'd like to enter a plea for sanity when it comes to school scissors here. People, we need to provide our schools with scissors that don't completely suck, and we need to replace them often enough that they are usable to the average child. I speak as a "righty" who repeatedly tried to use the left-handed scissors because they were the only ones that weren't completely worn out and dull. Frustration, thy name is school scissors.)

What makes a poorly functioning muscle sense really awful is that kids with this problem may assume that they are stupid because they can't do what other kids do. They may feel stupid, the other kids may call them stupid, their teachers may internally label them as "not really up to this class's level," and so forth. That's a potentially self-fulfilling idea that is rough on any kid. Or any adult.

No one wants to look stupid or spend time working on a project and then end up frustrated. These kids will often start avoiding anything that might challenge and stretch their poor muscle sense. This means avoiding any kind of play or activity that might end less than well.

For me, as a kid, this meant avoiding arts and crafts activities as much as possible from about fourth grade on. My ability to glue dried pasta to make art projects, to draw and cut out pictures, or to produce any kind of mobile, diorama, poster, or other craft-type project was just about nonexistent. Basically, if a project required a coat hanger or a shoebox, I was out of there as fast as I could be.

I felt pretty dumb, but there were actually things I was really smart at. One of them was reading. I could read at a pretty darn good speed with pretty darn good comprehension from an early age, and I loved to bury myself in book after book. It was my great escape from a world that didn't feel so good to interact with.

My parents were pretty shocked when, in seventh grade, I came home with a failing grade in my reading class. Reading. The one thing they absolutely knew I could do. I was immediately on the hot seat to explain how I could possibly have done such a thing.

So I explained. The teacher had given us the assignment of reading four 200-page books over the report period. She needed to make sure we had done the reading and understood what we had read. However, she taught reading classes for every single seventh grader in the school, which meant grading at least four book reports for each one of us. So she decided we were only allowed to turn in book reports in the form of posters, dioramas, and mobiles.

The month I got that failing grade, I had read *Gone with the Wind* in one sitting (with bathroom breaks). There are 960 pages in that one book alone. (I had read many other books, as well. I was readin' fool!)

If the teacher had objected to my choice of book owing to the racism and apologetics for slavery, that would have been understandable. But she genuinely didn't care what books I picked, what she cared about was getting a report that looked like I'd spent time and effort making something that represented what the book was about.

I don't remember my project for *Gone with the Wind*. I do remember that my project for Heinlein's *Time for the Stars* consisted of a half-dozen crude cutout rocket ships hung from a wire hanger by strands of yarn. It was definitely done at a first-grade level (if I'm being generous). It was flat-out awful.

Upon hearing all of this, my parents came to an executive decision: They would help me make craft projects for my reading class.

They felt it was right to help me because the teacher was grading a reading class on arts-and-crafts skills, rather than reading skills. They explained pretty firmly that if I flunked an art class because my projects were as flat-out awful as that rocket mobile, they would not help me with that.

Thank heavens my parents understood enough about what was going on to realize that it was absolutely not fair for my fine-motor planning to be considered the measure of my academic ability. I felt so lame turning in projects that I knew were dreadful, and it would have crushed me to actually flunk reading. Especially because I'd have had to take that same class with that same teacher again.

Thing is, my crafting skills did not have to be so very poor. It's possible for a child with a poor muscle sense to grow and stretch that sense and develop better and better skills. But because I was embarrassed by anyone seeing how clumsy and awkward I was at art skills (and physical skills), I avoided the very activities that might have helped me.

I was fortunate enough to have an art teacher just two years later who encouraged me to do things "wrong"; the fact that she encouraged experimentation and gave me great coaching meant I actually enjoyed art classes and even sometimes poster projects thereafter.

Kids with a poor muscle sense need safe times and places to develop their skills. Going through the same process of developing muscle awareness and coordination that everybody else does can take a long time for them. They need to be able to develop those abilities one step at a time. Often, the place to do this is with the school's OTs or with an OT outside of school.

The Basic Body Sense

The third and last of the unpronounceable and difficult-to-remember sensory systems is the *interoceptive system*. My spell-check really hates it.

If I refer to the interoceptive system, either in my own mind or when I'm discussing it with people, I usually call it the *basic body sense*—because it is the most basic body sense, more basic than any other.

This basic body sense gives us the most basic possible information about our bodies: How does our body itself feel? This is the sense that tells you if you are hungry or thirsty, whether or not you have a headache, and when you need to pee. In other words, this sense is vital to everything: mental functioning, physical functioning, social functioning, and, of course, simply staying alive.

When your basic body sense is off, the people around you can easily be bewildered, angered, or frustrated by your behavior when you actually aren't doing anything wrong. If you've got a super-sensitive interoceptive system, then a minor headache or normal hunger can feel like a sign of serious illness. If you've got a very under-responsive basic body system, then you can get pretty darn sick without knowing it, or ignore a really nasty headache that is a sign of something being wrong.

And, of course, there's the whole toilet training problem. Not only can it be difficult to teach a kid to use the toilet if he can't feel when he needs to go, but minor distractions can mean peeing himself well past the age when the other kids no longer do so. Not only is this embarrassing, it means missing out on fun activities and having everybody upset with you. The third time in a month that parents have to bring clean pants to school for their second grader, they are going to be pretty annoyed. Unfortunately, telling a kid he's too old for this and he really has to start paying attention and being more mature will not help his body and brain connect better, and the shame and embarrassment do not do anything for his neurological development.

Are there worse things than that? So glad you asked. There are kids who don't feel hungry. They just don't. Their bodies never, ever tell them that putting food into their mouths is an important thing to do, and if they find food tasteless or off-putting because of problems with other sensory systems, then they really protest when they are asked to eat. And if they have poor oral-motor skills as well, they may not want to have anything to do with food.

When you think about it, eating is a weird behavior. You respond to a feeling somewhere in your torso by putting things in your mouth, mashing them up with your teeth, and swallowing them. If you don't have a feel for it, if your body isn't actually telling you to feed your face, it must seem pretty silly, not to mention inconvenient and kind of gross. I mean, hey, you yanked some roots out of the ground and pumped some milk out of a cow's udder, and now you want me to actually put that stuff in my mouth? Are you insane?

Fortunately, most kids will eat something and will not completely avoid food. Kids who actually won't eat often has to have stomach tubes put in and go through some pretty intensive training from an OT—and Mom and Dad have to go through some training, too. It is tough, but these kids can overcome their problems, usually but not necessarily before Mom and Dad tear out every single hair out of their respective heads.

One point: Having a kid who won't eat or who has a very limited diet doesn't mean you're a bad parent. Unless you are actually poking your child with a pointy stick every time he picks up a piece of food, you aren't discouraging him. And the zillion-and-one child care books and pediatricians who assure you that if you wait long enough, your child will eat out of sheer hunger, simply haven't figured in an actual lack of hunger as a possibility.

Most of us with SPD have less spectacular but marvelously inconvenient issues with eating. Me, I've got a fun little thing where hunger, thirst, and fatigue all frequently register as ravenous hunger. If I get sleepy enough, I will eat everything in the kitchen because my brain is telling me over and over that I'm super-duper hungry. It has taken me roughly forever to get a handle on this.

At this point if I feel hungry I actually go through a mental checklist: When did I eat last? When did I sleep last? How much water have I had to drink today? Actually *thinking* about the facts of the situation can get me onto the right track.

And, I'm going to include this here, despite the fact that I've not read specific research on it: My ability to distinguish hunger, thirst, and tiredness has improved greatly as I've added more physical activity to my life, and seems to get worse with forced inactivity. As I'm writing this, I've been very limited for a few months by a particularly spectacular sprained ankle. It turns out that sprains can take longer to heal than breaks, isn't that fun?

This lack of physical activity for months on end has made me less sensitive to hunger and thirst, and that means I don't feel hungry or thirsty until I am totally starving or totally dehydrated. As you could likely guess, this is a problem.

So, yes, if your child who has SPD is not hungry all day and then is suddenly ravenous, he could easily have a wonky interoceptive system.

That basic body sense is so basic we don't even think about it, but most parents are familiar, often very familiar, with having to be aware of their kids' bodily functions. This is where the "Are you sure you don't have to pee?" and "You need to eat something" type conversations have to continue past the age where most kids would have these things pretty much down. More importantly, you have to teach your child to have those conversations with himself.

It took me until I was in my 40s to realize this: If I actually sit down and consciously think about each part of my body to check if there is pain, hunger, thirst, or other fun stuff going on, I can often persuade my interoceptive system to give me enough information to get by. It's one of those things where you get better at it as you practice over time. You can't learn to feel your own thirst, dehydration, or other inner-body feelings overnight, but you can coach yourself into getting somewhat better at those things.

Running Hot and Cold

There is another area we need the basic body sense for: knowing when we are hot or cold. There's a whole art form to this process, where the brain and body do some rather amazing communication to let us know when to take off our jackets or put on our gloves, and when we need to stay indoors.

Kids who lack this chunk of the basic body sense will go out to play with a coat on and simply leave that coat on, no matter how warm it gets—or go out in a t-shirt and shorts when it's freezing.

There is a difference between having SPD and just being, well, a kid. Some kids don't want to wear a heavy coat or other layers because they want to look tough. Apparently, we currently live in a culture where teenage boys in particular show how unbelievably awesome they are by wearing t-shirts when any sane person would go out in about seven layers of clothing. Some girls do the same, either to appear cool or because they have very specific ideas about what makes them look cute.

If your child doesn't pick up on hot and cold, this is again a job for an OT, but parents can help by finding a way to review the upcoming weather and discussing how this relates to clothing. That isn't as high-falutin' as it sounds.

You can make a big drawing of a thermometer and spend time with your child cutting out catalog photos of different kinds of clothing, adding arrows from the types of clothing to the appropriate temperatures as you go. A child can be reminded to look at said thermometer on a regular basis to figure out what he needs to wear. Working on the idea that different numbers mean different clothes and that the temperature is different at different times of day can be a useful support for kids who can't figure that out on the fly.

What a Pain!

Feeling sick, well, achy, or perky depends on the basic body sense. A stomachache can range from mild indigestion to extremely immediate full-on food poisoning, but if that basic body sense isn't on point, telling the difference can be nearly impossible.

There are a lot of kids who go to the school nurse almost continually who never seem to actually be sick. These kids are perceived as lollygaggers, wimps, or malingerers, but if that interoceptive sense is telling them that something is WRONG, then they are just doing what their bodies are telling them.

Combine that with the level of stress, frustration, and resulting anger or anxiety that kids with SPD can rack up on a daily basis and you've got a prescription for a kid who feels really sick almost every day. If you can't tell a stomachache that results from crushing panic from one that comes from a nasty virus, then you not only want to lie down or take five, you NEED to, because you don't know whether you are going to feel better after a 5-minute break or be suddenly subject to serious diarrhea and vomiting. Your gut may be mildly off, but your body can still be telling you that you are absolutely not well enough to sit upright. It's confusing as heck, and what makes it even more weird is when other people blame and label you because you simply have no idea what is actually going on with your body.

It is hard, tremendously hard, to learn to read those body signals better when you are being teased and blamed. If all of your energy is drained by either making attempts at self-defense or feeling serious shame for your failure to manage this, you don't have the energy left for tackling the underlying problem. And, of course, a child guessing on his own won't know what to do or how to do it.

Kids who can't tell when they are sick at all, who have a very poor ability to even notice the signs of illness in their own bodies, are often seen as tough or as having a good work ethic. It's less likely to get them immediately teased or condemned, but it's more serious. Lying down for 10 or 20 minutes because your stomach hurts is nowhere near as dangerous as continuing activity when your body is actually suffering.

There is a custom in our culture for helping adults who don't recognize or respond to their own bodies' signals of illness; we assign someone to tell them, repeatedly and firmly, when they need medical attention. These signalers are most often called "wives." But it's not a perfect system, and kids need help from an OT and understanding parents to get good at telling when they are really hurting.

Both reactions to internal pains are exaggerations of perfectly useful traits. A person who is super-sensitive to pain will be more likely to work out ways to do tasks more safely and less stressfully; a person who is less sensitive will be able to focus on physically stressful tasks without being distracted by temporary body signals. The range of "normal" is pretty wide here, but if a child is outside the range of safety, then the problem needs to be addressed.

The Basic Five

N ow that we've dealt with the trickier, less well-known senses, here is a review of the standard five senses that we were all taught in school. I'm going to try to provide a little bit of info about how these senses are affected by SPD; I'll go into a lot more detail in the following chapters about the specific types of SPD.

Hearing

We all know something about disorders of hearing. For example, we know that there are people who are deaf, partially deaf, or who can't hear really high or really low pitches. None of those issues has to be present for a person to have a processing disorder affecting their hearing.

As in the example of "cocktail-party hearing," being technically able to hear something and actually hearing it are pretty different things. There can be a big difference between what you *can* hear and what you *do* hear: A child whose hearing seems normal when he is tested may still have serious difficulties picking out one voice from many sounds or hearing those sounds correctly.

Hearing tests are usually done with headphones in quiet rooms, and for most of them the child only has to focus on one kind of sound at a time. Testing conditions are very different from eating dinner with the family, sitting in a classroom, or being on the playground.

If a child is super-sensitive to sound, he may seem to overreact a lot in the classroom. A kid with hypersensitive hearing and perfect pitch may not behave well when the bell rings, because school bells are noisy, jarring, and not even close to being in tune. If this kid gets labeled as a behavioral problem (because he gets upset and angry when sounds hurt his ears) it can affect his ability to function at school. It can be just as bad to be labeled a "sissy" or a whiner if he simply complains when harsh sounds are really painful to him. Pretty soon he can learn that his pain doesn't matter, and that adults can't be trusted to believe him or help him when he's really hurting.

Some kids have difficulty distinguishing sounds: They can hear the full range of pitches and different kinds of sounds, but they can't make out some of the important details.

In my case, while my hearing tested perfectly, I didn't have the ability to distinguish between what are called "plosives" very well. Plosives (that's not a misspelling, it really is a word) are sounds like the "T" sound or the "P" sound, where instead of using your voice, you use your mouth itself to make the noise. That "P" sound is made with the lips, not the vocal cords, and was very hard for me to hear when I was a child. In fact, I had no idea that those noises were actually different from each other until I had rather a lot of speech therapy.

I'll talk about how my speech therapists taught me to hear better in Chapter 7, "Journeys in Sound and Sight."

Seeing

Seeing may be the most important sense for humans in our modern society. There are many important signals that are purely visual, from simple stop lights to that look your mom gets when you're arguing and she's almost but not quite mad enough to ground you so you only have a few seconds to start behaving before you'll rue your sass.

There are some good, basic eye tests that are administered to most schoolchildren. The illiterate "E" test, where children have to identify the direction a capital "E" is facing, is pretty darn useful and tells us a lot about children's vision—but not everything.

As with hearing (and all of the senses), there is a wide variety of potential problems with seeing and SPD. Some kids are very oversensitive and are overwhelmed easily by the chaos of bright colors that is the typical first-grade classroom. Other kids seem to hardly notice their visual surroundings.

There is also the problem of the child who has only recently been found to be severely nearsighted or farsighted. Some children can almost immediately take advantage of the improved sight that comes with having glasses that give them clear vision, but some kids with SPD have a really hard time adapting to suddenly being able to see so much more than before. If a kid has had years of bad hand-eye coordination because he is terribly farsighted, the process of getting eyes and hands synced up can take time and may require help from an OT or behavioral optometrist.

Oh yes—the behavioral optometrist, the best friend of the child with severe visual processing problems. This professional is, like any optometrist, a doctor of optometry, who has to be licensed just as any physician does and may have a degree in a second, related field, such as psychology.

My own brother had severe behavioral problems in nursery school, none of which seemed to make sense. He generally seemed more interested in colliding with and physically hitting other kids than playing with them. He hit other children when he had no apparent reason for doing so, and all the standard behavioral interventions didn't do squat.

It took an examination by a behavioral optometrist to find out that he had double vision. His eyes were slightly crossed and so he saw double images of everyone and everything. He started hitting other kids simply because without making physical contact, he couldn't tell which image was real and which was a visual mistake without making physical contact.

And now, I will briefly interrupt this section on the visual system to share a quick word on problems in the diagnostic process.

The optometrist told my parents that little boys with this problem usually hit people a lot, while little girls use hugs and affection to figure out what is what. The only problem there is that it takes a lot longer for little girls to get screened and diagnosed with vision problems because they aren't getting themselves kicked out of nursery school. They're just considered affectionate, or clingy.

While this book isn't about how girls and boys wind up getting diagnoses at different rates and at different stages of development, I feel it's worth a mention here. This problem is a small part of why we are so far away from having simple ways to screen kids to determine if they need a full SPD evaluation (never mind ADHD, learning disabilities, autism, and so on).

If you have had a really hard time getting to the point where you know your child has SPD and are able to start figuring out what he or she needs, I just want you to know that you're in the same boat as everybody else. It doesn't take a long time to get a diagnosis because you aren't observant enough or don't care enough, it takes a long time because we don't have very good ways for spotting these kids yet. The boy/girl differences are just one of many issues that make diagnosis super-tricky.

End of interruption. Back to vision.

My brother underwent vision therapy that made a huge difference. For a long time, he had to wear special glasses that had partially blacked-out lenses to permanently train his eyes to look forward correctly. But the initial therapy made a huge difference in his behavior quite quickly. He stopped his pugilistic habits and became much easier to deal with in a lot of situations.

But the teachers at the nursery school he'd left didn't believe it at all. And when he went back, he started up the old patterns again. The combination of the setting and all of the teachers being completely sure that he was a deliberately violent child was too much for a little kid to take.

Smell

Humans often don't think much about how their sense of smell affects them every day. Oh, sure, we know we can smell the difference between a good perfume (like Channel No. 5) and a noxious toxin (like Axe Body Spray), but we don't identify individuals by smell as many animals do.

Yet we all know how powerful smell can be. Familiar smells can take us back in time, like when we smell cookies baking and it brings back childhood memories (or memories of the time we spent working in a particular bakery, either way).

When I get a very faint whiff of stale cigarette smoke that has permeated furniture or drapes, it sends me back to my Nana and Pop-Pop's house. It has to be just a faint whiff, because my Nana cleaned house like she breathed: constantly. A stronger scent takes me elsewhere. That small difference in the intensity of a smell isn't just something we humans can distinguish, it can be the difference between feeling warm and fuzzy about a smell and feeling like "I've gotta get out of here now!"

Smell is a lifesaver. We know rotten food is rotten by the smell—whether it's eggs, milk, or fruits and vegetables, the smell of food that has past its prime is instantly recognizable. There are a lot of college students who would willingly risk eating nasty food rather than throw it out, but a strong enough smell can deter them and save them a lot of pain.

Long before the food is so rotten that its appearance is off-putting, we can smell that it is nasty and think twice about eating it. Our noses are that sharp.

Of course, there are many thousands of other good and bad smells that we respond to without even thinking about it. Over time, our brains can change how we react to specific smells as we learn what they mean.

Even more useful is our ability to screen out smells that are constant so we can then tell if a new smell pops up. When I worked at Bloomingdale's bakery (back in 1985, when that particular Bloomingdale's actually had a bakery), people would ask how I could stand the constant wonderful smell of fresh-baked items, and I answered them honestly: After the first month, I didn't smell it anymore. My nose and brain had come to an understanding so that I no longer had a conscious awareness of that background smell, and therefore was no longer distracted by the odor of cookies and croissants.

Other people make even more important adaptations. People who work in close contact with sewage systems eventually (partially) screen out the stench enough that they are able to work without constant barfing. Even more important is the fact that once they've adjusted to the normal nasty smells, they have a much better ability to pick up on any anomalous smells, which can help them find problems.

If your sense of smell isn't filtering very well or is overly sensitive, problems can result. There are kids with SPD who not only refuse to eat new foods, but they react to them as if they were really disgusting. And for those kids, those foods actually are disgusting. They aren't just being drama queens (well, no more than any child is).

The big cause for all that food disgust? The brain and nose have gotten together and determined that a food has the wrong smell for food. That kid's internal meter is telling him that this is bad, very bad—the same way your internal meter would tell you that a rotten egg was very bad. The kid isn't merely being fussy; his brain is stuck in a mode that won't let him see that food as edible.

Of course, the opposite problem can apply. A kid who is super-duper insensitive to smells may find food bland and unappetizing. Smell and taste work together, and if the sense of smell is lying down on the job, that can mean the food tastes like nothing. Cornflakes in milk can seem like just a bland sludge, so that particular child won't settle for anything less than Sugar-Coated Cocoa Bombs (Now with real sour gummy marshmallows!).

Smell alone doesn't always account for a limited or eccentric diet. Another part of that is our next sense, taste.

Taste

Clearly, having an extremely oversensitive or undersensitive sense of taste is going to affect your eating habits. And that means SPD can affect your eating habits in a big way.

Normally, most people raised in similar cultures will have similar or at least heavily overlapping food likes or dislikes. It would be unusual to introduce a young child to his first piece of chocolate and have him respond as if it were a dead mouse. It would also be unusual to give a child his first taste of a real lemon and not have him pucker up so adorably you just have to post a picture on Facebook.

Also, it's normal for kids to refuse some foods some of the time. It's unusual for people to like all foods all of the time, and most people have days when they feel less like eating than others. Head colds and sinus allergies can have a big effect on what things taste like, and that can mean having a suddenly (and temporarily) "difficult" eater. And some days some kids are just plain ornery and don't want to try something new.

When a child with SPD has processing problems that affect taste, he can be tremendously fussy about what he eats or simply have very little interest in food. A child who is very undersensitive to taste is likely to see foods that are even slightly bland as gross and tasteless. A child who is oversensitive can be overwhelmed by strong flavors and refuse to even touch foods that have been found wanting in the past.

Of course, eating behaviors are more complex than just taste issues. There's that whole basic body sense thing—how well the body and brain are syncing up on hunger signals can have a huge effect. And if something smells icky, it is very hard to get to the point of ever tasting it. Your nose guards your mouth, so to speak.

As always, you can't fix an SPD problem with a purely behavioral approach. Behavioral stuff does help when it's used in a way that is realistic about the child's abilities and limits, but you can't bribe or punish a child with serious taste processing problems into eating foods that his palate is screaming for him to avoid.

My mother nearly went nuts trying to get me to eat a more varied diet. I was great at eating the standard set of American meat products (beef, chicken, pork, turkey, and lamb) and would willingly eat most fruits and many different grains, but veggies and I were not on speaking terms. Naturally, Mom wanted to change that.

Then she came across a new technique in her reading. It was a simple approach: If you put a small serving of a disliked food on the child's plate and then just let the child know that he will not be allowed to leave the table until he eats that serving, eventually the child will get bored of sitting there and eat the food. This is somehow supposed to lead to the child more readily trying and eating new foods. Really.

One night at dinner, my mom put a smallish serving of cooked carrots on my plate and told me that I could not leave the dinner table until I ate them.

Long story short, Mom caved a few hours after my bedtime. I would have lived at that table for a month before I ate cooked carrots.

This plan was doomed from the start because it didn't take into account the fact that I could no more force myself to eat a small serving of cooked carrots than to eat a small serving of roofing tar.

Mind you, Mom had deliberately picked a food that has a pleasant taste to a huge portion of the population. Hey, they're carrots—they're brightly colored and sweet and full of nutrition. Bugs Bunny swears by them. She was trying not simply to get me to eat carrots, but to show me that new foods could be pleasant.

But cooked carrots taste awful to me. They hit a whole lot of senses at the same time: When I had cautiously touched a little piece to my tongue, it tasted nasty to me, but just as vital was the texture, which was a weird combination of firm and mushy, and the smell, which I simply didn't like. In fact, it is largely because of the texture that to this day, I really hate cooked carrots. I'm pretty good with raw carrots, despite the fact that they take a prohibitive amount of chewing (yep, it's an oral-motor issue), but the cooked ones? Ick.

(I'd like to take a quick opportunity to apologize to the carrot farmers of America. I know you grow a popular, tasty, and nourishing crop, which is enjoyed by millions. The problem that makes me hate carrots is considered a neurological disorder, not a good thing.)

My mom couldn't make me eat something I hated by using this approach because my sensory apparatus was telling me that this food was inedible and bad. If I had tried to force myself to eat them, the result would have been barftastic.

Nice try, though, Mom.

Touch

The sense of touch is, for my money, the most seriously complicated and significant sense, especially when it comes to SPD.

Touch seems pretty straightforward. Come to think of it, when touch works, it is pretty straightforward. Touch works two main ways: through being able to sense and learn about objects via touch and through being alert to what's happening to our bodies via the skin.

The skin you're in is one extremely large sensory organ, which means a ton of constant input. Just wearing clothes or feeling the air moving past the skin that isn't covered by clothes means constant input through the skin of the entire body. Every bit of the skin is in touch with something, even if it's only air, all of the time. That's a HUGE amount of data to process.

Usually, the brain and the skin work together in a way that means we humans don't even think about texture of our clothing or a gentle breeze wafting past, say, our naked arms when we wear short sleeves. Typically, we don't go around feeling our shirts or socks against our skin all day. Most folks go from wearing a long-sleeved shirt one day to a short-sleeved shirt the next without ever thinking, "Wow, I can really feel that air moving past my forearms!"

You know what's coming. The ability to ignore our socks once they're on, the ability to comfortably wear different clothes that provide different coverage on different days, the simple ability to walk around without thinking about the air moving across our arms, those are all things that come with good sensory processing.

With SPD, it is possible to be acutely aware of one's clothing. The classic example is the child whose behavior changes drastically with her clothing. She might be a little angel when wearing old, soft, comfortable jeans but can be an absolute nightmare on days when she's been stuffed into something frilly with lots of itchy lace.

Temple Grandin, PhD, talks about this in her book *Thinking in Pictures*. As a child, she was incredibly sensitive to wearing scratchy petticoats, which felt to her like sandpaper rubbing against her legs. And like me, she hangs onto old undies and tees until they are completely unwearable, because the process of breaking in new ones involves running them through a dozen wash cycles before wearing them even once.

Having an oversensitive tactile sense can make new or different clothing seriously painful and can have a profound effect on things like choosing clothes and even picking furniture. Rough material on a couch can mean that a child can only sit well if he's protected by worn, soft jeans and socks.

Touch is also one of the senses that helps us tell where we are physically. When SPD causes *undersensitivity* to touch, it can mean that the child feels out of touch with his body and the world. There are adults with SPD who wear tight elastic on their wrists and ankles as often as possible to help them locate themselves.

As implied above, there are actually two kinds of sensations that come from touch. There's what's called the "discriminative" touch system, which gives us input about what we are touching. For example, a person who is buttoning his shirt is getting constant feedback as to which parts of his fingertips are touching smooth buttons and which are touching the texture of the woven cloth.

Discriminative touch is important to a lot of things other than just buttoning clothes. Tasks as different as holding a pencil, changing the car's oil, and kneading bread dough depend on getting good information from our skin to do the task correctly.

That means the tendency to feel pain from what most people would consider ordinary touch and textures can affect learning and behavior in a lot of ways. The oversensitive child may feel pain from holding specific types of pens and pencils, while the undersensitive one might not be able to get a good grip on his pencil because he can't really feel where it is.

The other kind of feeling and information that comes from touch is just as important. That's the "protective" sense of touch, which alerts us to sudden touch of all kinds.

Protective or alerting touch is something we respond to totally automatically. If an insect lands on your arm, you probably just shake or brush it off immediately, without any thought at all. Your skin tells you it's there before you even see it, and you get rid of it. You don't need to think about whether there are biting or disease-carrying insects known to be in the local area, you just get rid of the potential problem.

A kid who has a form of SPD that affects this alerting kind of touch may not be aware of these things. It may not seem like a big deal to have a bug walking around on your arm and never notice it, but it is important to know when you are being touched. A child who ignores repeated taps and pokes when a parent or teacher tries to get his attention can easily get labeled as a problem kid. Not fun.

Having an oversensitive response to this alerting kind of touch is not fun either. For a very large part of my life, I often overreacted to a tap on the shoulder to an extent that did not work out well for me. I'd chew people out for touching my arm while I was busy, because my brain interpreted that light touch the way you would interpret having a knife put to your throat. To me, it was a flight-or-flight situation, because the processors that interpreted that touch in my brain wrongly signaled that there was huge danger.

Eventually I got into enough trouble for yelling at people over being startled that I worked very hard to respond in a calmer way. There were only two problems: (1) I could not always keep my response relatively calm, and (b) my internal response was still complete panic, which meant I was then on edge and likely to lose my temper on a slightly delayed basis.

Mind you, I don't know whether I got the worst of this particular area of sensory processing problems. It seems to me that it could be much more dangerous to not respond at all to a real tactile threat than to overrespond. Either way, it's not fun to have an out-of-whack connection between your tactile system and your brain.

So there you have it, all eight sensory systems. Those three "insider" senses, the sense of gravity, the muscle sense, and the basic body sense, are just as important as the Big Five that we were all taught about in third-grade health class. And all of them can be affected by in a pretty wide variety of ways by the various types of SPD.

Chapter 6

Types of Sensory Processing Disorder

I've been talking about SPD in general, but there is actually a group of specific subtypes of sensory processing disorder. Unfortunately, these tend to have awkward, somewhat technical-sounding names, and I don't have any clever substitutes. However, they are all simply different ways in which our ability to deal with the input our senses give us can be severely screwed up and massively inconvenient.

The descriptions of SPD and its symptoms are all related to problems that *most* people have *some* of the time. People can be physically oversensitive or insensitive to sensory input some of the time because of things like lack of sleep, poor diet, illness, or stress. And people do have little quirks about what they can and can't tolerate. That's not what we're talking about here.

Dr Lucy Jane Miller, who knows more about SPD than anyone, points out that SPD is *chronic* and *disruptive*. Those two words represent the difference between a temporary or minor problem and a real disorder, so they are important.

Of course, being chronic and disruptive makes the difference between having an occasional problem and a disorder in many different situations and not just in people with SPD. A kid who gets a headache from tiredness or stress and needs a few ibuprofen tablets and a short break maybe once a month is in the typical range; a kid who gets actual migraines on anything like a regular basis needs intervention.

Like headaches or other problems, SPD can be continuous all day or only start at a certain time of day, or under a certain kind of stress. If every time your kid tried to practice his handwriting he got a genuinely splitting headache, you'd know something was going on, right? You might take him in for a checkup or to the optometrist to have his vision checked, because you'd know there was a real problem.

SPD works the same way. If it's constant, frequent, or interfering with your child's ability to learn, it's worth checking out, and it's worth being persistent to find out what your kid actually needs in the way of support to be able to do what kids do.

Notice to Parents: You, as a parent, know your child better than anyone. If she is having frequent and troubling problems, if she can't get through an ordinary school day, if she is depressed or anxious to the extent that it interferes with things like learning and playing, then there is more than just a quirkiness going on.

The following information should help you if you are undecided about getting your child assessed for SPD, and it is also designed to help you understand and think about your child's diagnosis if she already has one. I want to support your search for help for your child and also support your ability to think clearly about what is happening in your child's life.

As far as the technical-sounding, jargon-y words go, please remember: You don't have to memorize every word. If you are working with a teacher, therapist, or OT who uses more jargon than you can handle, let them know. Please do ask as many questions as you need to for you to understand what they are saying.

(In fact, that goes for teachers, therapists, and OTs too. If you are a professional working with other professions or with parents and they use unfamiliar language that you find hard to follow, ask questions. Do what you need to do to make sure you understand what is going on.)

Remember, all of this jargon is just a convenience to make talking about SPD quicker and easier. It is not an IQ test and if someone can remember and use the jargon better than you can that does not mean the person using it is smarter than you are or understands your kid better than you do.

Starting with Sensitivity

There are a bunch of issues and categories that come up with SPD, and some of the most common ones are fairly straightforward. Over-responsivity and under-responsivity mean what they sound like: a person could be really, really sensitive and responsive to any or all of their senses, or a person could be really, really insensitive and seemingly oblivious to one kind of sensory input or another.

Any sense can be individually over- or under-responsive, or a child can be over- or under-responsive in an overall way, so that he is almost always or very frequently affected by sensory input in a way that just doesn't work.

These two kinds of SPD are among the biggies, and they are usually grouped together with a third kind, which is "sensory craving." Sensory-craving kids can't get enough input, are all over everything, and seem to get more worked up the more they touch/taste/paw/knock over everything.

Together, these three kinds of SPD constitute a group called "sensory modulation disorder."

Sensory Modulation Disorder

Sensory modulation disorder (is there an echo in here?) is an overall term that describes a broad spectrum of difficulties in processing information. It's sort of like what would happen if your cable connection or satellite dish was working fine but your TV's volume and video were out of control. You could have perfectly good input to your TV and yet have sound blasting out or at a bare whisper, with video that was blurry or jagged or insanely bright. You'd be frustrated as heck, and you'd probably get new TV but if, instead of your TV it's your brain that is processing input in a crazy way, you can't just replace it.

That's what sensory modulation disorder can be like. There is plenty of good input but no way to make it usable. It's super-frustrating and confusing.

The first kind of sensory modulation disorder is the previously mentioned sensory over-responsivity. Actually, "overresponsivity" is usually written as one continuous word, but I have difficulty reading it that way, so I'm typing it in a way that is convenient for me and that emphasizes the key part of the word, "over."

This is sensitivity and responsiveness over and above normal processing. When a kid has sensory over-responsivity, he can find the whole world to be "too loud, too bright, too fast."

This kid may be picking up even the tiniest sounds, so he has trouble responding to his dad's voice because he can't tune out the sound of the air conditioner or the hum of the microwave. He gets in trouble for not listening, which makes him upset and on edge, and the stress and adrenaline make him even more over-responsive, to the point where he can't eat dinner with the family because the sound of forks scraping on plates is agonizing.

There are many possible problems resulting from over-responsivity. Maybe an ordinary tap on the shoulder or another kid slightly bumping him can startle this kid into a full-on fight, flight, or freeze moment—even to the extent that he avoids other kids to avoid that painful state of panic.

Circumstances that might seem perfectly safe to you, like being in a room full of kids working independently on craft projects, can be overwhelming if you are painfully alert to all of the random, unpredictable sounds and movements. Being overwhelmed in this particular way can overload a kid to the point where he can't function, melts down, or simply shuts down completely.

Me? I've got some serious over-responsivity problems. It is truly a royal pain, because it is not completely consistent. Usually I find what they call "coffee hour" after a Sunday service pretty tough, but I can hang in there and even carry on some amount of conversation despite the room being full of moving, talking, eating, and otherwise less than quiet people.

After 30-60 minutes of chatter, I'm pretty much ready to keel over, and I could really use a break. I'm often completely exhausted after a few hours of social interaction (being with other people in any way, shape, or form) because of the constant need to consciously make myself focus on the right input source (like the person who is talking to me personally).

Yesterday, I was involved in a conversation in an area that I had not realized was going to be the location for a chili luncheon. Chili is one of those smells that takes serious work to cope with, and I actually had to end a conversation by simply saying, "I have to go now" and walking away with no other explanation. It's not the best social response, but absolutely necessary.

Yes, having my sense of smell triggered by something painful to me made it harder for me to hear. The body and brain chemistry of stress can make the senses go off one after the other, like some kind of insane domino effect.

But in the above situation, I got to walk away. If you're a kid in a classroom and over-responsivity has you overloaded to where you can't function, much less control your own actions well, you can't just walk away. You just have to keep trying to tough it out, desperately trying to pretend to do what the other kids are doing so you don't get in trouble, right up to the point where you are simply in too much pain to cope. And that's when you'll act out (or shut down) and quickly find yourself in hot water, utterly unable to convince anyone that you were doing your best and just couldn't keep going.

Over-responsivity often manifests as a very defensive kid. He is constantly in that defensive state to protect himself from very real pain, and his brain will automatically take the actions that stop that pain. Your brain will usually try to help you in that way: avoiding things that can cause pain is simply normal and instinctual.

He may want to have more friends or play with the group, but if he makes friends with another child that person might assume it's okay to tap him on the shoulder or start an ordinary, low-level play-fight, or even come up to him with loud enthusiasm over something super-cool. Any of those might cause his nervous system to go into overload, so it's way safer to be as prickly as a cactus, standoffish, or a "snob" so as to keep people at a distance.

Sensory Under-Responsivity

Sensory under-responsivity is, in a way, the opposite of sensory over-responsivity. I say "in a way" because it can look very different, but it's another case where "problem behaviors" happen simply because they are the normal, instinctual actions of someone who is processing input in a bad way.

Sensory under-responsivity occurs when a child's brain takes a while to even notice what's going on. This kid may not consciously notice sensory input that everyone else in the room is aware of.

The teacher goes to the board and tells everyone to take out their books, and the under-responsive kid is still engrossed in looking out the window or finishing up the last task, completely unaware that anything else is going on in the classroom. Eventually she notices what's happening, but it will take her a while to figure out which textbook to open and what page the class is on. She misses a lot of stuff.

Sometimes under-responsive kids seem to be kind of "floppy." You try to put your kid's socks on and it's like wrestling with a wet noodle. There's no normal resistance, the child simply isn't able to respond to what you are doing; his body is still in a neutral, uninvolved state. He's technically awake, but he's not really awake.

(***Note:*** Poor muscle tone can sometimes also be an indicator of problems other than SPD. There are infections, autoimmune disorders, and metabolic disorders that can have poor muscle tone as a symptom. As always, it's good to bring this up when your child has a checkup, and if your child has always had good muscle tone and then loses that tone, definitely have your pediatrician give him the once-over.)

Under-responsivity can look like laziness or noncompliance, but it is more pervasive and keeps a child from doing things he has no reason to avoid. The child is taking in information too slowly to keep up, and he misses a lot of vital stuff. If you took 5 or 10 or 20 seconds to actually process the first of a list of instructions given out loud, would you be able to follow all of the instructions? You'd still be dealing with the first few when you were expected to be halfway done.

Under-responsivity can show up in a number of ways: Maybe this child slowly becomes aware that someone in the room is speaking or that all of the other children have gone on to the next task. Or he may not notice that all of the other children are already waiting in line for recess and the teacher is waiting for him (trust me, if you make the other kids miss the first 30 seconds of recess just once, you will never live it down—never, never, never).

These kids can be under-responsive to the most basic needs of their own bodies. This child may be slow to notice that it's really too hot out to keep his jacket on—or he may not realize it at all and become dehydrated, cranky, and difficult because his brain never alerted him to the "I'm hot and sweaty and need to cool down" signal.

This kid may have a lot of problems with his classmates. When the other kids are playing catch and the ball accidentally goes his direction, he probably won't notice it or engage his body to stop it until after the ball has rolled into the street and down the storm drain—even though the other kids were yelling at him to grab it.

The other kids may think that he's dumb or annoying. The teacher may think he's not too bright and can't cope with the regular class work—even if he's really bright and just needs enough distinct input and rousing activity to wake up and take in the information he needs.

Mixed Responsivity

But wait, there's more! Before we get to the third major category of sensory modulation disorder (which is called *sensory craving*), there is a key issue that happens with under- and over-responsivity. Mixed responsivity, in which those two things come as a package deal, is probably the most common combination of two different types of SPD.

Yes, a child can be over- and under-responsive at the same time. Sometimes this means that different senses have different problems: A child is super-sensitive to sounds but seemingly indifferent to varying flavors of food. Or it can be a constantly changing jumble. The key here is that the kid's data processing is wonky, and he needs help to get his brain organized. It's like having a broken thermostat: the house may be too warm sometimes and too cool at others, but the underlying cause is the same.

Mixed responsivity is one cause of the classic "nerd" move of panicking when the ball is hit toward your position in softball. At first, you can hardly tell where the ball is, because your delayed visual tracking can't keep up with the fast-moving ball. The other kids are yelling at you to catch the darn ball, but you may not understand why they are yelling until it's too late—or you may panic from the sudden sound of people yelling at you.

Suddenly, your overly alert sensors tell you that the ball is coming straight at you right this second, and your entire nervous system goes into panic mode. You can't fight, you can't flee, but you can freak out, and you do. The resultant ducking, flailing, and general panicking will then inevitably result in much mockery, bullying, and (if your team loses) some serious blame. Your chances of being picked anything but last plummet, and you feel like an idiot.

Yet all of that ducking and flailing is not something these kids (including, of course, me) have control over. Their nervous systems are doing the best they can, but they need serious help to get to the level of organization and coherence where they have a chance at catching that ball—or at least making a grab in the right direction instead of throwing their hands over their heads while ducking wildly.

This kind of responsivity results in just as much, or even more, rage and confusion than the other types. No, I'm not talking about the rage of other kids or the child's teacher, nor yet the parents: I'm talking about the kid with SPD herself. If you genuinely can't react any other way to that softball headed your way, you feel angry. You get angry at yourself for being an idiot; you get angry at the other kids for expecting the impossible of you; you get angry at the gym teacher for setting you up for failure and humiliation.

For me, if other kids were playing without me and the ball just happened to go in my direction, their behaviors made me confused and enraged because I could not make any sense of their behaviors—and they couldn't understand mine. As soon as kids notice that the ball is going out of bounds, and there's another kid nearby who isn't playing, they yell stuff like, "Hey, McIlwee, heads up!"

The idea there is that the kid they're calling out to, in this case me, will retrieve the ball and return it to them so they can resume play without having to chase the ball. It's only polite for the bystander to do so, but for me it was an impossible situation.

There I am, walking around the playground, trying to pretend that either the other kids didn't exist or I didn't exist, and suddenly, out of nowhere, I heard my name being screamed. Panic attack, panic attack, panic attack.

There was no way for me to understand that those other kids were not purposely being hurtful. To me, there was no other possible response to someone unexpectedly demanded that I retrieve a ball than a panic attack, so obviously, they were just trying to make me have a generally problematic freak out.

A panic attack meant it might take hours for me to feel anything like normal. I knew I was going to be twitchy and miserable when I went back inside, and that every little sound or movement was going to set me off, so that I'd probably stay panicky all day.

And how could they not know that informing me that their sporting equipment was in my vicinity wouldn't do any good? I simply couldn't visually track the ball fast enough to get it before it was way, way, way past me.

So when someone yelled, "Hey, McIlwee, heads up!" I took it as an attack, because it felt like an attack and made my day suck. In that full-on burst of adrenaline and misery, I might well scream at the person who called my name, angry because they had frightened me to pieces for no reason—because obviously there was no way that them yelling was going to result in anything but me having the aforementioned freak out. I mean, did they actually think I was going to spot and retrieve the ball? Had they met me?

And then there's the aftermath of knowing you are the kid who can't even figure out where that ball is, much less retrieve it before the other kid does. You know, the other kid who is reluctantly jogging after the ball because he had met me and knew that there was no way McIlwee was going to get to that ball before sundown.

Mixed sensitivity: the overly sensitive audio panic button combined with sloooow visual tracking. And they wondered why I would do stuff that got me kept inside during recess.

Sensory Craving

Sensory modulation disorder comes in a third distinct flavor: sensory craving. This is also called "sensory seeking" or, less officially, "How do I get my kid to stop licking people and running head on into solid objects?"

Yes, there are sensory cravers who lick stuff way past the toddler stage— and those who grab everything, can't sit still, can't focus on any one thing, and can't keep their hands to themselves. Sensory cravers demonstrate all sorts of behaviors that get them seriously negative labels. These kids are often called *problem children, overly aggressive, rebellious, irresponsible,* and *disobedient,* because they will seek new and varied sensory input so constantly that it is more than one parent or teacher can do to keep up with them.

These kids are seemingly addicted to input. Sometimes they run from one toy to the next or from one room to the next almost frantically. They may use more senses to examine objects than is called for—that is, they smell and lick and grab stuff that most children their age would be able to simply handle and look at.

Does every kid have moments like this? You bet! If the situation is a first trip to the county fair, many children may run around touching and smelling and ogling everything and anything.

Sensory craving, on the other hand, means this happens all the time. One thing that sets sensory cravers apart is that they get more disorganized, more wound up, and often more frenetic as they get more and more input. Running around like a nut will make a sensory-craving kid even more jumpy. Handling everything in the classroom or on the playground seems to increase this child's need to move and grab, so that when you finally make him sit down he is brimming with nervous energy, and it doesn't take long for him to be in trouble again, whether it's rocking back in his seat or drumming on his desk.

So sensory cravers seeking input are doing what their brains and bodies are endlessly pushing them to do, but they seldom seem to get the kind of input they actually need to focus. The round of running from one piece of playground equipment to another, smelling and grabbing and swinging and yelling, doesn't wear them out so that they can sit still at last.

These kids may not even stop when they should be worn out or when they are doing something sedentary that they really like, such as watching a TV show that they enjoy. They may chew their hair incessantly or interact loudly with the characters on TV. Even when they are tired, their nervous energy drives them on.

And these kids can suffer huge social consequences when they get to be too much for other kids to handle. They play rough, even when the situation calls for gentleness, and they interfere with other kids' games by grabbing toys or just plain running across the play area in the middle of playtime. They are not good friends with kids who like to line up dominoes in carefully laid patterns.

One key here is that these kids seldom, if ever, mean to be unkind or interfere with others. They are remorseful when they accidentally hit or upset other children. They are genuinely unaware of the damage they are likely to do until it's too late.

For these kids, trying their hardest to sit quietly simply doesn't work. Doing little or nothing isn't in their natural range.

Most importantly, these kids can often calm down and get organized if they get involved in physical activities that are specific and directed at a goal. Running around the playground just winds them up, but carrying a box of toys out from the classroom, stacking chairs, or otherwise doing useful tasks that are hard work (not too hard for their age and size) can have a real positive effect.

This means that giving them specific physical activities with clear goals can make a big difference. If your kid goes 15 different directions between the car and the house but can get it together for a least a little while if he is clearly instruction that he must help carry in the groceries, he might just be a sensory craver, and he might need a lot of structure and challenge to get through his day.

It seems like all the random sprinting in the world can never wear out this child, but start-stop patterns like a brisk round of musical chairs or relay races can really get him to focus on his movements and get his body and brain in sync.

When I say these kids can get it together with organized physical activities, the emphasis is on the ACTIVE part. Standing in the outfield and waiting for one's turn to bat are definitely not the activities of choice for these kids. Working on a "personal best" 100-meter dash (or whatever distance is age appropriate), on the other hand, is a great way to burn off excess energy while developing a sense of self-efficacy.

As always, each child is different. One kid may get totally mentally and physically "organized" by playing *Dance Dance Revolution*, while another may just get wound up. You've gotta figure out what works for your kid the old-fashioned way: trial and error. As with all forms of SPD, this is one of those situations where no one person can solve every problem. A trained OT is a great person to bring in—ask if she's dealt with sensory-craving kids before.

This is a situation where harnessing the energy and power that are hidden underneath a pile of problems and bad behaviors can make for a particularly awesome kind of awesomeness. There are a lot of successful adults who are high-energy, physically active people. It isn't a matter of changing who this kid is underneath: It's all about harnessing that energy and drive so that this child can learn to use his get up and go instead of being batted around by every impulse like a pinball.

This is also a situation where you might want to invest in that mega-jumbo bottle of ibuprofen. And, your child's teacher might appreciate one as a gift during the holiday season. These kids are tough to parent, but they have so much to offer that it is well worth it.

Sensory Motor Problems

Dyspraxia. Wonderful word, sounds very interesting, kinda science-fictiony, but what does it mean? It refers to problems in the area of "praxis." (Fill in your own Carnegie Hall joke here.)

Praxis is the process of planning and doing some kind of movement or task. It's a process you usually don't think about: When, for example, do you actually think about having to put one foot forward and then the other to walk? If you have a pretty decent level of praxis, you never think about motor planning, even though children have to develop this complex skill over years—even decades.

Take the following: A 12-month-old is crawling around the kitchen and spots a delicious piece of doggie kibble on the floor in the corner. She crawls over to the kibble, picks it up easily, puts it in her mouth, and enjoys eating the kibble, lint and all—unless, of course, Mom or Dad has spotted her and forcibly wrested the treat from her grasp.

This seemingly mundane and normal set of 1-year-old actions involves three different sets of motor skills! That little girl has had to use her large or "gross" motor skills to get across the kitchen, her fine-motor skills to use the smaller muscles in her hand in a precision movement required to pick up the individual kibble, and her oral-motor skills to successfully chew and swallow it. It took untold millions of years to evolve creatures capable of finding and eating a linty kibble, and it is no minor thing when it happens.

All of the above means dyspraxia is a Big Honkin' Deal, so let's talk about it in a bit more detail. Dyspraxia (I really like that word) happens when a kid (or adult) can't gather and use knowledge about his surroundings and himself to actually get things done. The relationship between where the ball is and where he swings the bat is not simply a little off—it's pretty much non-existent. The relationship between how his hands move and what he's handling may be pretty iffy. Even the ability to walk through a room he's been in a zillion times can be problematic, because his brain can't necessarily do the motor planning he needs to walk where the furniture isn't.

So you get a lot of labels with dyspraxia. Kids who are actually smart can get labeled as clumsy and stupid by their classmates—and by adults. Most adults don't say it as often or as loudly, but there's always that one family member who thinks it's hilarious to point out that little Hermione's legs don't seem to know where her feet are.

Let's talk for a minute about how dyspraxia looks and feels from the inside, and how it can be helped.

Large-Motor Skills

Kids with poor large-motor skills are usually way behind their age group in ordinary tasks like running, hopping, and being able to put the ball in the basket. This means difficulty getting a hand- or foothold when climbing the jungle gym, difficulty riding bikes, difficulty dodging in dodge ball, and generally being picked last in gym.

In case you haven't been through it, being picked last or next to last every time you break into teams is serious torture. Think about it: You stand there in a line with allllll those other kids, and they get picked one by one, gradually, while you wait. You know that while most kids get picked according to their athletic ability, some get picked for their popularity, and some because their friends want to be on the same team with them. You see the cluster of newly picked teammates huddle around each captain as he picks more players, and all of those kids are giving advice and pointing out kids they want to have on their team.

Sometimes they talk about you as the pickings get slim. They point and whisper frantically not to pick McIlwee—she always drops the ball. The line you're standing in has been whittled down to a sparse group, and you all look at each other, knowing full well one of you is going to be last. And all of you hope it isn't you this time.

I've been picked last after kids who had physical injuries got picked. I've been picked last after kids who had colds, or who were sniffling and sneezing from allergies. I've been picked last after skinny kids, fat kids, and kids with all sorts of appearances that might be associated with not being very good at sports.

When you can't coordinate your limbs because you have poor large-motor skills, you get picked very, very late in the selection process. Sometimes the other kids will argue about who gets stuck with you, as in, "We don't care if you have more players than us, we don't want her." So very not kidding.

Why am I talking about the social effects of dyspraxia here? Because dyspraxia affects the whole person. SPD isn't just something you treat with occupational therapy, speech therapy, and sensory diets. SPD and dyspraxia hit the unsuspecting SPuDster in many areas, and the later chapters are going to deal with that. So I'm trying to set up some super-important stuff here.

A kid with poor gross-motor skills is not just going to be frustrated that he can't do stuff he wants to do, he's also going to be frustrated by how everybody sees him. And there is a good chance he'll buy into the idea that he is not as good and worthwhile as other kids are. It's not fair, but it's what happens.

Gross-motor skill problems can interact with other SPD stuff in weird ways. I had a hard time learning to hit a ball with a bat, but my Dad practiced with me with a whiffle ball and bat and then a regular softball and bat. Just plain practicing can sometimes help, if it's with supportive people and isn't too intense. I got to where I could contact the ball with the bat, albeit not square on.

But I didn't get much farther than that because my over-responsivity tripped me up. When I actually hit a real baseball with a real bat, it hurt like crazy. It was the equivalent of someone smacking my hands as hard as they could with a two-by-four. I wanted to be better at playing games, I wanted to gain acceptance, but it hurt too much. I couldn't even imagine how the really good hitters could possibly stand to smack the ball hard enough for a single, much less a double. Ow. Ow, ow, ow, ow, ow.

Practice did help me get a bit more coordinated some of the time, and often low- or no-pressure practice, where a kid is led along gradually toward a goal, can help a kid with poor fine-motor skills. Just getting out and having a catch with my dad was great, because he didn't have any ego tied up in it. Neither did I as long as there were no other kids around.

Obviously, practice is less helpful when a parent or other relative has an emotional stake in how well a kid does in sports. If Mom is deeply invested in her little girl being on the tennis team like she was, said little girl will pick up on the fact that Mom is constantly evaluating her. Same with the dad who wants his son or daughter to hit home runs, or the grandparent that feels that a "real boy" is good at football.

The worst? Well, some little league or kids' soccer leagues feel that play, exercise, and good sportsmanship are key. Others, not so much.

When you're the uncoordinated kid, those parents who take every game oh-so-seriously are not your friends. Anyone who is shouting at the coach to take you out because you are a lousy player is going to hurt you, yes, but when, instead of another kid mocking you, it's a group of adults it's worse. Soul-crushingly worse.

There has been a lot of research in the field of social psychology that shows that people who are good at something will do better when they are being watched—but people who are bad at that thing will do significantly worse when they are being watched. Give your kid the chance to play in a no-stress zone.

I started seeing much bigger improvements in my gross-motor skills than I can ever remember having when I started working out in my own at home with videos and books for instruction. If it's just me and the TV, I can take the time to figure out how to do things right and gradually improve—really! Since I was 40, I've gotten a lot better at all of that stuff because I started working on my strength and endurance slowly and gently all by myself. It turns out that I will push myself pretty solidly when there's no one to compete with but me.

The other thing is that by doing research and going slowly, I force myself to do things correctly, which is huge. When I was a teenager, if I tried to do pushups and sit-ups, I had no idea of what muscles were actually supposed to be involved, and I hurt myself. I needed more info and less pressure so I could figure out where the heck my abs are and how to get them to actually not be completely inert. Hey, I don't need abs of steel, but it's nice to have abs that I can locate and use a bit.

I still bump into stuff a lot more than other people, but my ability to tell my limbs what to do and have that thing actually happen has gotten way better. And that's me being in my 40s. As in, you can improve this stuff at any age.

This is one of the many, many areas of SPD where getting an OT who likes and gets along with your kid is important. My relationship with my dad made it possible for me to hit a ball and have a catch, and while there is no substitute for playing with your kids, an OT that your kid trusts and feels confident with can help a ton and a half.

Fine-Motor Skills

Kids who have SPD often have poor handwriting or difficulty using utensils as God intended (stabbing your brother with a fork does not count). These are areas where SPuDsters often (but not always) fall behind in fine-motor skill development.

Unfortunately, fine-motor skills are a huge part of how children are judged. Children with bad handwriting are often considered to be slower mentally than kids with lovely handwriting. Learning cursive is not just a test of fine-motor skills, it can be a precursor to how every teacher judges your intelligence. Heck, if you take long enough to simply print numbers on the page you can flunk a math test purely on the basis of your fine-motor abilities!

Fine-motor skills are also part of how people are judged in the cafeteria, in arts and crafts, and eventually in business lunches and on dates. Being able to eat without drawing any attention to the actual eating process is important. For some reason, no one notices if you eat in a perfectly polite way, but if you can't hold onto your fork they get all judge-y really quick.

This isn't just about using the hands to do things like handwriting or using a fork—it's not just a matter of operating the many tiny muscles of the hand in concert. Those are important skills, but these problems involve a lot more than just the hands.

When you write, draw, eat, or otherwise use your hands to do stuff, your upper body is completely involved, your posture is involved, and your tummy muscles, which are now known as your "core," are involved, too. If you can't sit up very well or you get tired of holding your head up, it is hard to write neatly. If you can't keep the paper from wandering off without resting an entire arm on it, that's also going to slow you down.

In other words, a kid who has poor fine-motor skills won't get far in improving them if he can't be gradually led into activities that give him some upper-body strength and better posture. This is an area in which you have to look at the entire person, because just finding and implementing ways to improve fine-motor skills won't work if the other parts of the body aren't able to support that hand.

My fine-motor skills were often "meh," but they were seldom spectacularly bad. As with so many things, kids will find workarounds to get things done. My solution to my fine-motor issues when I was a child was to be *as tense as humanly possible* whenever I had to write or draw. Seriously tense. Muscles super-tight. I had an iron grip on my pencil/crayon/pen at all times, and my upper body was rigid too.

I managed to have decent handwriting, but my path to get there worked against me in so many ways. To control a pencil I would have to hold onto it incredibly tightly and lean hard on my left arm (I'm right-handed), both to pin down the paper I was writing on and to keep my hand in the correct writing position. My left forearm was planted on the table, which meant I would write with my hand in increasingly cramped positions until I finally actually moved that forearm enough to straighten my wrist for a little while. With both arms planted, I would write for a while, get my hand all cramped up, then move both arms and the paper to start the cycle of lameness again.

When I started college, the amount of time I spent taking notes with a pencil suddenly became huge, which meant having constant pain in my hand from my deathlike grip. It wasn't until then that I learned they make these little gripper-things that you can put on your pencil to have a bulkier thing to grip. Wonderful items. Much less painful. You can get them for your kid. You can also get them for you.

One of the main jobs parents, teachers, and OTs have is to find ways to get a kid with fine-motor skills who are in pain, out of pain. It's really hard to learn to write or do anything when your hand and upper body hurt. No one is enthused about practicing stuff that hurts.

This is an area where I do want to let you know that a person can survive even if her fine-motor skills do not become excellent. It is great to do all you can to help a child become better at something that is basic and useful, and I would greatly encourage parents to be gently persistent in this area, but perfection isn't necessary.

Not every kid gets all that good at everything. In my case, I worked incredibly hard on my fine-motor skills, often for months on end, and guess what? It didn't entirely work out. No one is good at everything, and finding my limits actually helped me feel good about myself.

When I was in grade school, the magician Doug Henning was the most awesome human being alive under the age of 50, and I wanted to do magic. I got the standard magic kit and a passel of library books, and I started practicing.

It took me months to learn to do a simple penny drop in an adequate manner. If "penny drop" doesn't mean anything to you, it's the classic trick where your grandfather takes a quarter out of your ear. 99% of grandfathers can do it, and many of those are a little arthritic. As a 10-year-old and again as a 16-year-old, I spent untold hours trying to get it right.

I also spent an insane amount of time learning to palm a card. That's what it sounds like—you've got a playing card in the palm of your hand but it looks as though your hand is empty . It isn't all that hard, but my hands had only two settings, completely limp or incredibly tense, so it was always blatantly obvious if there was a card in there.

I was pretty bummed that I couldn't learn to do slight-of-hand, but it was fascinating to try, and I love to watch close-up magic to this day. I can't do it but understand the principle, which makes it somehow more thrilling to watch.

Also, at some point I picked up Penn and Teller's books and therefore learned a few tricks that require very little coordination. If you want to do the same, just remember that the fork-in-the-eye bit does not always go over well with folks who have heart problems.

There were also the 2 years I spent trying to learn to play guitar, which was basically more of the same. To this day, I can't move my left hand from one chord to another without doing it one finger at a time, and I can't strum without watching my right hand constantly. Basically, it just didn't work.

Why am I including my stories of abject failure here? Because I want you know that humans can have big flaws and still live well. What I actually needed was not the dexterity of a master, but rather to be able to write things down well enough that I and other people would be able to read them. At this point, I can even write in the dark, so I can jot down all of my brilliant 3-AM insights without so much as turning on a light. I don't actually need to be able to do all sorts of slight-of-hand, and there are other people who are filling the world's need for great musicians. I'm good at other stuff, and I'm good with where I am.

By the way—when you get to the point where you can write in the dark easily and clearly, you learn one great truth: That thing you think is a brilliant idea at 3 o'clock in the morning is almost always "Vanilla hogshead monkey monkey small Lego figures for everyone." Remember that always.

Oral-Motor Skills

This is a really rough area for some of our kids. Many folks don't realize that difficulties with speaking, chewing, sucking on a straw, or swallowing can come from lack of coordination—and coordinating the lips, tongue, and jaw so that they work together smoothly is pretty darn tricky. Some kids need serious help from a speech-language pathologist or an OT (or both) to get that set of skills down.

This kind of SPD can make it hard for babies to suckle, and then follow it up bay making it hard for them to learn to deal successfully with both mushy and solid foods as they get older. Mind you, all kids have some difficulties learning to eat, and all kids make horrible messes and blow mashed-split-pea bubbles with their goopy, baby-food-laden spit—that's typical. What's not typical is being unable to get through and past that phase while all the other kids are chowing down on bits of cold cereal and cut-up hotdogs with gusto and coordination.

This is when what they call "feeding issues" arise. It's hard to be enthused about eating when you can't get one darned Cheerio to go down the right pipe! It is actually natural for a kid who can't get the chewing and swallowing thing down to get frustrated and be super difficult. It's hard to be urbane when eating is a constant struggle.

Some kids who have poor oral-motor development often have their mouths sagging open and do significantly more drooling than is typical for their age. This is incredibly rough, because both adults and other children will often think they aren't very smart. The clichéd stereotypes of being "slack jawed" or "drooling" are applied to these kids all too often.

Oral-motor problems can interfere with speech as well. If you're a typically bright kid who has a bit of a drooling problem and can't speak very distinctly, it is really hard to show your strengths and knowledge to other people. A child who is having a hard time in this area may be more than a little frustrated with the human race!

Me, I got lucky on this one; while I was apparently born with a full compliment of SPD as well as Asperger's, I didn't have any real oral-motor problems—but I did experience similar frustrations, so when I run into a kid who is having a little mouth-coordination problem I always try to listen longer and better and pay attention to what she is trying to communicate rather than how she is communicating it.

Even more than speech therapy and occupational therapy, these kids need to be listened to in situations where no one is rolling their eyes or running out of time and patience. They also need chances to eat when no one is looking at the clock or counting bites, so they have a chance to focus on what they are doing and maybe even what tastes good instead of feeling the constant pressure to eat neatly and quickly.

If you take a kid who is frustrated by his own inability to speak clearly and find a good speech therapist who likes kids in general and him in particular, really good things can happen. If you take a kid who struggles with eating and swallowing and pair him up with an OT who he can tell is an open, friendly, trustworthy person, he's got a great chance of moving forward and learning to use his own body better.

This is yet another situation where practicing skills is important, but having a safe and possibly even fun place to practice is key. I'm emphasizing it here because children who struggle with just getting their mouths to work often don't get the credit they deserve. These kids can often wind up feeling dumb and incompetent when they really just need a good solid boost. We can't afford to let any of these kids be undermined by hackneyed ideas about slow speech and a so-called "slack jaw."

Posture Pals

There is another kind of sensory motor disorder out there, one that is different from any other form of SPD. It's called "postural disorder," and it hits kids right in their midsections. That is to say, it's mainly (but not completely) about the muscles of the abdomen and trunk.

In my own head and when I'm giving a talk, I usually just call this "posture disorder," because that's what it is. And what posture disorder is all about is having key areas of muscle weakness and uneven muscle strength. Stuff that we do everyday—heck, stuff that we do almost every moment, like sitting and standing in a stable sort of way—involves the strength and endurance of a whole bunch of different muscles.

This is another one of those problems that involves a system that is so simple and basic to everyday functioning that most of us are seldom even aware of it. Most of us never think about the fact that when we are simply sitting upright, our core and back muscles are doing serious work. These muscles have to be strong enough to keep doing the same work continuously for hours on end. Sitting up in a chair or on a stool is serious work for the body—and impossibly hard work for kids who have posture disorder.

Since this is called "posture disorder," it's no shock that the most common and obvious problem these kids have is poor posture. They tend to rely heavily on the arms and the backs of chairs, they often rest the weight of their upper body on their desk when drawing or writing, and they are very likely to be limp and languid.

These kids are big on activities that can be done when slumped in a chair or sprawled on the floor. After school, they may form-fit themselves to the sofa so that their sitting-up muscles (which are super fatigued from the school day) can have a break.

Obviously, developing more muscle strength through physical activity is very helpful for a kid with a posture disorder. Not so obviously, forcing a child to exercise without doing your research and consulting a professional is likely to do more harm than good.

First and foremost: When a child has a posture disorder, he has learned the hard way that physical activity is not for him. He often dreads or resents the activities he associates with exercise, like needing to stand upright and alert for long minutes as an outfielder. He loses at sports, thinks the Wii Fit is flat-out torture, and tends to think of the playground as a good place to find something to lean against. He is absolutely not up for a rollicking half-hour of doing planks—or any other form of physical fitness.

If you take a child for whom exercise is a horrible experience and force him to work out, he will feel like 5 miles of bad road both emotionally and physically. And he will be pretty sure you hate him because he's a weakling/sissy/lame-o. Why else would you do that to him?

This means that a kid with postural disorder has to be led gently into physical activities that will help him develop strength. An occupational therapist (or possibly a physical therapist who has the right training to work with kids) can help him start at a level that is only a tiny bit challenging for him, so that he gradually develops a bit of body confidence and can start enjoying some kind of mild physical play.

There is a second key reason that just doing sit-ups is not the solution here. Most of us never notice or think about the way different sets of muscles have to pull or push against each other to create good posture and balance.

You need core strength to sit up straight, but if your abs were all super-strong while your back muscles couldn't contract right back at them, you'd slump forward instead of sitting up straight. Weak muscles that have to work with and against strong muscles are a problem.

For example: If you're like most people, when you kick or lift your leg, your abdominal muscles contract automatically to keep you steady. It's just a thing your body will do, one more convenient service it offers to help you through your day.

It's been some decades since it was first discovered that many people with back pain lack this useful contraction. That is, some people do not have that helpful, useful automatic contraction of muscles in the trunk. They lift a leg and their abs say, "Whatever."

Upon realizing that back problems were associated with poor abdominal contraction, very smart people realized that developing more strength in the muscles of the trunk might help some of the people who have back pain. But there was one problem: If people focused solely on strengthening those key abdominal muscles there was a backlash (so to speak).

Turns out, if you strengthen just the front part of the torso, you don't get rid of back pain and problems. Having really strong abs to contract when you stand is great, but not if the rest of the torso muscles don't do squat. You need your abs to work with your back and side muscles, not against them.

This has a huge implication for kids with posture disorder. It means that just doing exercises to strengthen specific muscle or sets of muscles can be a real problem—especially because people with posture disorder often already have out-of-balance muscles.

An OT can find ways to turn a child's likes and interests into active play—and active play engages more muscle groups than sit-ups or calisthenics. If a child is playing at being a turtle and staying low to the ground to do so, that means engaging a whole bunch of muscles in a natural way while avoiding any fears that child might have about being unsteady and slumping or falling over.

And a good OT can add to or tweak the play process in a way that gets the right muscles working—the turtle may get a chance to go up a ramp or to "eat" blocks or pull into his shell and slowly poke his limbs and head out again.

Making play of exercise and making sure different muscle groups get the chance to work against and with each other again and again can be a real chore, and if an OT is available to make that happen, take advantage of it.

You can also use some of the tips in this book to bring the child slowly into physical activities and help promote a mentally healthy attitude about his posture disorder. If he sees it as a problem that can be tackled a little bit at a time, instead of as an innate failing that will always make things hard for him, he will be less likely to develop or hold onto any ideas about being stupid, slow, or otherwise faulty just because he can't keep up.

Sensory Motor Problems, Recapped

We've got a lot of kids in this world who need extra help to learn to use their bodies. These kids need assistance and support to learn to tackle the important tasks of childhood (and of life): learning, working, and playing. It is absolutely possible for parents and other adults in a child's life to make a big difference in that child's ability to simply use his own body to get things done that will help him be happy and useful to himself and others.

Muddy, Fuzzy, and Indistinct: Sensory Discrimination Disorder

Sensory discrimination disorder is the term for one of the trickiest, weirdest, and (for me) most problematic little neurological glitches ever. It's not about intensity—it's all about making sense of input.

It's possible for a child to hear every sound around her and yet not be able to make sense of the words. There are kids who go through life hearing much of what is said as if it were spoken by an adult in a Peanuts cartoon special—"Whaa whaa whaa whaa, whaa whaa whaa whaa."

There are kids who can touch and sense both the button and the fabric on their shirt just fine, but the two things feel exactly alike. They know what's there, but they can't tell what's what.

Sensory discrimination disorder is all about the meaning of the input, rather than the input itself. It's very frustrating when you can detect input but can't get meaning out of it.

For example, I have always had some problems with my basic body sense (you may recall it's technically called "interoception"). This means that while I was growing up, I often felt strongly that something was wrong but didn't have any idea what it was.

When I say I felt something was wrong, I mean that I thought something was wrong in the world: Someone was not doing their job right, a teacher was being unreasonable about a project, my mom was asking too much of me, or other students were being total jerks to me.

All of those things can really happen—heck, all of them really did happen to me, and most of them happen to every kid at some point. If you suddenly feel like you are under a disproportionate amount of stress and your interactions with others are suddenly just too much to take, it's pretty natural to look for the problem in the people around you.

The teacher whose tone is suddenly much more annoying than it's ever been or the parent who has just recently asked you to do a few more things than usual seems like the source of the stress. And there was always one kid or another who was getting to me at school, because kids.

Sometimes all of that was actually happening: People around me were genuinely doing something that stressed me out, whether they were asking too much of me or making changes to things I was comfortable with. It happens.

But sometimes after about 2 or 3 days of hating the world in general, I would suddenly have a really bad cold, at full force. At no time did I feel like I was "coming down with a cold." I just knew that something was very wrong and couldn't make out what it was.

Similarly, I've had several days of frustration with the world around me suddenly give way to a severe toothache. Getting the cavity filled would result in a much less antagonistic relationship with the people around me, and the feeling that the world was against me would disappear.

Let me say emphatically and clearly: This does not mean that every kid who is having problems with the people around him or who is getting angry, frustrated, or just plain fed up with one person or another has a physical illness. SPuDsters are human beings, and humans have problems and friction in their relationships. If you're a teenager, for instance, the friction is pretty much nonstop.

Also, physical illness is less frequent in the life of a child with SPD than real interpersonal problems stemming from adults not understanding how much SPD can affect a child's day-to-day capacities.

But for me, being able to locate and verbalize physical pain was a very tricky problem when I was growing up and for a lot of my adulthood. I had to work hard at developing better communication with my body to be able to check out my physical feelings in a better way. And in doing so, I've been able to deal with other humans more sanely. Usually.

There still are definitely times when I knew something's wrong somewhere in my body and yet have great difficulty locating it. During the healing process after getting that nasty sprained ankle, I had a heckuva lot of difficulty pointing out to my doctor the exact spots where the pain was still significant. As in, I knew my foot and ankle hurt like crazy, but I had to sit down and carefully, very gently move, tense, and prod the hurt area to be able to accurately verbalize or even point out what was going on.

In Every Sense

Sensory discrimination disorder can happen with every single sensory process. It's an interesting exercise to think of some of the ways we depend on our sensory processing to make incoming data from every single sensory system into something usable.

It is possible for a child with sensory discrimination disorder that affects her sense of touch to have tremendous difficulty distinguishing textures, so that all the fabrics and fasteners of her clothes feel too similar to distinguish—or many of the objects around her feel the same, same, and same. Next thing you know, you've got a kid who is frustrated when dressing herself, and also at arts and crafts, where distinguishing between things that are being glued together is one of the key skills.

Reading books depends on being able to feel the pages; you need good communication with your fingertips to distinguish one page from another and to tell whether you've turned one page or accidentally turned several together. It's also necessary to know how much force to put into turning pages, so you don't rip or crumple them when you are way past the age where board books are acceptable or even interesting.

There are some unexpected areas where having sensory discrimination disorder that affects the sense of touch can cause a child great frustration. If the touch sensors inside the mouth can't feel the difference between different textures of food, the child attached to that mouth may have difficulty eating, because how the heck is he supposed to know when food has been chewed enough to be swallowed? If the texture of a whole piece of carrot and a chewed-up carrot feel the same, mealtime can become anything from a hassle to an all-out Heimlich situation.

And if a child's sense of taste is muddled and indistinct, food may not have much appeal. Or he may need food to have a very distinctive taste to be able to make sense of it at all. He could eat sour gummies by the pound but has no interest in, say, potatoes or veggies. (That, by the way, is when you bring out the jalapeño peppers. Hey, it's a vegetable!)

Me, I've got a delay in my sense of taste. I found this out because I sometimes get something different than what I expected or ordered. When that happens, that first big glug of iced tea tastes exactly like the diet cola I was expecting, which lasts for a second or two before I realize that, hey, that's not right. It's as if my brain fills in the flavor based on memory, until my taste processors actually catch up.

A muddled or fuzzy sense of gravity can result in a lot of falls and generally clumsy behavior. After all, when you lean over in your chair, your brain and body have to keep very good track of how far you can go before gravity is too much for you and you just flat out wind up on the floor. And it's even worse if you know you are starting to fall but can't figure out what direction to move in to correct it.

An "off" gravity sense paired with a muddled muscle sense is just as big of a pain as you'd think it is. I felt stupid every year when we did gymnastics in gym class, because I didn't dare ask the questions I wanted to ask: "Once

I'm moving, how do I tell where my legs are? How do figure out how much energy goes into jumping so I don't clobber myself on the dad-blamed horse every time?"

And, of course, I've already told you about some of the problems that arise when the basic sense of what's going on inside your own body is fuzzy. My case is pretty mild, but there are kids who can only vaguely sort of tell that they are getting a body signal when what body is trying to say is that they need to use the toilet. That's one of the most unfortunate issues, because kids who have "accidents" get teased horribly. Learning to locate and inter-pret the input their body is trying to get into their brains is pretty important at that point. So is helping them understand to the best of their ability that it's a wiring problem, not a personal flaw. That's one of those things where you've got to work on the emotional and social effects, just as much as you need to find an OT who has experience with poop and pee issues.

Every single thing that the sensory organs do for us can be thrown off by sensory discrimination disorder. It can be frustrating for parents and children alike when this part of basic development is shanghaied by a neu-ral glitch or three. But there are ways to help, and there are people who can make a huge difference.

I have significant sensory discrimination disorder in the audio realm, and some pretty annoying visual processing snags, and have been super-for-tunate to find ways to make up for these data-processing problems. It turns out you can use your conscious brain to help you hear and see more clearly and coherently. In my case, a huge amount of dumb luck, plus some obser-vant and knowledgeable adults, came together to do some offbeat versions of things that are now being done formally to help kids with SPD.

Journeys in Sound & Sight

I'm pretty sure that none of my speech therapists knew that they were teaching me to hear. When I was a kid, my hearing tested perfectly, but just being able to hear the right range of tones in the right range of decibel levels is not the same as being able to hear what people say.

In first grade, I was singled out for speech therapy because my "plosive" sounds were, as previously mentioned, lousy. My pronunciation of the sounds made by *T, P,* and *K* were extremely mushy and indistinct. My *B, D,* and *G* sounds were also pretty lame. I was clearly never going to find employment on *Sesame Street*.

What no one seemed to notice was that there was a very specific reason I couldn't pronounce these consonants clearly: They all sounded alike to me. Because I couldn't hear the differences between the sounds, I couldn't say them correctly.

Fortunately for me, my first speech therapist was an expert at teaching kids to hear better. She may well not have known that was her role in my life, but she did a great job.

Yes, a lot of the sounds in the English language were "fuzzy" in my brain and came out just as fuzzy when I spoke. My speech therapist spent lots of time showing me how to make those sounds.

She showed me how the sounds looked by demonstrating how to make them in an exaggerated way. She spent time getting me to imitate her, so I learned exactly how my lips and tongue should move when I said them. She showed me diagrams of exactly where my tongue should be in my mouth to make the sounds. I'm pretty sure she had a plastic model of a mouth and used that to illustrate her points as well.

In other words, I had a speech-language therapist who showed me over and over again exactly what those sounds LOOK LIKE. She was enlisting my conscious mind to do the things my unconscious data processors weren't doing in my brain, such as distinguishing between a *P* and a T.

At the time it all seemed to me like nothing but fun. I got to leave class to say silly sounds like "eepee" and "ootoo" with a grown woman and then practice making silly sounds on a daily basis when my parents went over my assigned pronunciation exercises after dinner. Less time with my peers, more time with my parents. It was great.

Without even trying, I was learning a lot about how the human mouth and face look when pronouncing all of those tricky sounds. Everyone around me was happy that my speech was clearer, but they didn't realize how important it was that my ability to interpret speech was skyrocketing!

When my speech therapist showed me over and over how to form specific sounds, when she showed me detailed diagrams and had me make those sounds while looking at my mouth in a mirror, she was setting up an ideal feedback loop. Every time I was looking at someone's face while they spoke, I was able to know what they were saying because of the shape of their mouth—and that meant I was getting constant reinforcement for my ability to hear those sounds.

Think about it: P and T sound much alike to me, but they don't actually sound totally exactly precisely alike. If I saw a person's mouth say "T," then my brain was both able to know what they were saying and also to get a little bit of data: "This sound is a *T*, not a *P*. *T*'s sound like *this*."

102

I had 9 years of speech therapy; 9 years of helpful and pleasant therapists who painstakingly taught me how sounds looked and therefore helped me learn to hear. Year in, year out, I got active coaching in my worst sensory area. It was genuinely insanely great.

It could have been pretty rough for me if I had never had that intervention. After all, with my innate, untrained listening skills, the phrase "totes adorbs" would sound exactly like "potes abords." No one wants that.

I should mention that even though I started speech therapy when I was 5 or 6, my hearing is still imperfect. I know I still have a large dollop of sensory discrimination disorder, partly through formal testing, and partly because I still don't have the "translate" function in my hearing.

Let me explain that. I have a friend who is wonderful. She has a doctorate in speech pathology and does research about helping nonverbal kids with autism to speak. She is also a Korean-American, and her name is thus Korean.

The first time I met this remarkable woman, she told me her name (naturally enough). And I couldn't hear it.

I asked her to say her name again, and then a few more times. After that, I felt I should stop asking because I felt it would be rude to the group we were in at the time if I kept belaboring the point. I had a vague feeling that her name had an H and a K in it somewhere, but really could not hear what she was saying.

Her work and knowledge were so impressive that I contacted her soon after and asked if she would meet me for coffee to discuss her work. She graciously agreed, and when she arrived, she greeted me by my name—but I still didn't know hers.

I asked her to pronounce her name a few more times, but I realized that wasn't getting me any closer to hearing it. Since there's no point in me ever trying to be cool, I just said outright, "Can you please write down your first name phonetically? Because I have no idea what it is."

She was quite happy to comply and after she wrote it down and then went over it with me slowly a couple of times, I got it. Her name was (and is) HyeKyeung.

The difficulty I had hearing HyeKyeung's name is the result of not "translating" sounds automatically. The average American would hear her say "HyeKyeung" once or maybe two times, and they would think, "Her name is HaeyKeyoong." That is, they would hear the sounds right, but automatically substitute the standard U.S. vowel sounds into the name so they could hear and say it naturally.

The fact that the Korean language vowel sounds are said quite differently than American vowel sounds meant I literally couldn't hear her name. My ears heard the sound, but it meant nothing as far as the language and speech bits of my brain were concerned. The word was a complete blur until HyeKyeung was nice enough to (literally) spell it out for me.

So my speech therapists did a lot to help me learn to hear sounds, but there are sounds they didn't teach me, and I still run into little problems sometimes. Since that very happy day on which I was diagnosed with Asperger's and thus found out that I have SPD, I've been able to work out ways to get around those problems. Problem solving is a lot easier since I've got a good understanding of the problem!

But hearing speech is hardly the only kind of audio processing humans need to do. When it comes to hearing other things, like music, I got very, very lucky.

Music Is a World within Itself

Music is amazingly powerful stuff, and it has the ability to affect us emotionally, socially, intellectually, and probably in a bunch of other ways I'm just too thick to notice. One of the best things about music is that hearing it makes people want to learn to make it themselves.

I've already talked about my useless attempts to get my fingers to cooperate with actual guitar playing. In my childhood there were also failed attempts to learn piano, viola, and drums. Some of the smartest and nicest teachers you can imagine futilely tried to get me to work those instruments correctly, and I learned a lot from them.

Yes, I learned a lot from teachers who absolutely could not teach me to play musical instruments. Early on, I chalked this up to my own lack of practice. I was excruciatingly embarrassed to practice piano, because all of my mistakes were audible to practically everyone in the house. Later on, I tried guitar and practiced for untold hours in the confines of my room, where any wrong sounds I made were relatively unlikely to be heard by others.

It turns out that spending multiple hours practicing guitar every day for 2 years made me exactly as good at playing guitar as I was at playing piano, which is to say, I can't play at all.

I even went to a high school that offered "music major" classes for people who intended to go on to study music in college. I took every music class I could jam into my schedule, which meant that in my junior and senior years, I was taking seven units of music a week in addition to choir practice. I received training in sight-singing, reading music, following an orchestral score, and conducting, in addition to vocal lessons.

The result? Nada. Still can't read music, still can't play music. I can carry a tune (most of the time), but overall I have exactly enough musical talent to know that I have no musical talent.

Turns out that all of that work did great things for me anyway. All of that reading and studying and practicing taught me how to *listen* to music. I'm pretty sure this affects hearing other things, as well.

Learning to follow an orchestral score means learning to hear the instruments both separately and together. Reading obsessively about various types of music meant I could bring knowledge with me when I heard music, making it more meaningful and resonant.

An aunt gave me a book about the Beatles when I was perhaps 12, and I read it repeatedly before I listened to most of their albums (the sole exception being *Abbey Road*). This helped me make the leap to hearing rock and pop music at an age in which I had previously been more interested in old radio shows than in what was actually on the radio.

I read about music while listening to music. I sat down and reread everything I could lay my hands on about a given Beatles album or Gilbert and Sullivan operetta before, during, and after listening to it repeatedly.

I wanted to be a musician. I listened to a whole lot of kinds of music, read about music, tried to play music. When I applied to colleges, I applied for engineering programs but secretly reviewed music programs via course catalogs. (I thought double-majoring would be great. Tell that to any engineer or music major and they'll bust a gut laughing. Words cannot say how hilariously ill-thought-out that idea was.)

I am now deeply, deeply grateful that for many years of my childhood and adolescence, I wanted to make music enough to work on that goal. I learned to hear so much through that process that I cannot see any of it as a wasted effort.

Learning to know music with my conscious brain led me to be able to hear words and music, both separately and together. Clearly, it is possible to have sensory discrimination disorder and still grow and learn far beyond the initial borders of that SPD diagnosis.

And to this day, I am the best damn air guitarist ever.

Warning: Your Mileage May Vary

This book is about understanding SPD, and in large part the means to understanding is rooted in stories of what worked (or didn't work) for me as I grew up with SPD. These stories are not meant to push a specific technique or program of treatment. Instead, they are about how and why certain things worked and, very often, about basing therapies on what children enjoy and love.

In other words, learning about music worked for me because I loved and was fascinated by music and had access to people, books, and records that supported that. If your child also has an auditory processing problem, this does not mean that pushing him into music lessons, classes, or long hours of required listening will help him hear better. In fact, for some kids with audio issues, that would be enormously frustrating or even painful.

I was lucky to find things that naturally interested me that, in the long run, benefited me a lot. If your child loves music in general or some kind of music in particular, do encourage that, but don't think a rigorous music program is necessary or workable for every child.

I say this partly with my first piano teacher in mind. The poor man was teaching a child for whom coordinating her hands separately was impossible and who got frustrated very easily. I had no idea how to transform what he was teaching me into playing the dad-blamed piano, and that meant a tantrum and/or meltdown came as a free gift from me to him with every lesson.

The poor man was patient and thoughtful, and he put up with a heckuva lot. He was a talented teacher and pianist, and if my mom had any idea of what a monster I was to him, she would have pulled me out of lessons in a trice, in addition to making me apologize and I don't know what else. I'd probably still be in time out.

So (*a*) don't torture a child who isn't suited to it with music lessons and (*b*) don't torture a teacher with a child who has developed neither the fine-motor skills nor the self-calming skills to allow the teacher to make it through a single lesson without having to deal with a giant hairy cat-fit.

Seeing Is Believing: A Work in Progress

I'm still learning to see.

My vision always checked out just fine when I was a kid, and even now, I have great vision through the magic of reading glasses. WHOOOOOOHOOOOO!!!! LET'S HEAR IT FOR BIFOCALS!!!!!!

Seriously, I love my bifocals.

Bifocals or no, I grew up having a lot of trouble "seeing" visual details. My vision was fine, but I had a pretty severe inability to recognize children's faces. This meant that in first and second grade, most of the other kids looked the same to me. It was really tough to pick out one face from another, and that can be socially disastrous. When the teacher says, "Jennifer, give the crayons to Erin," and Jennifer has no idea which of the other kids Erin is, that's pretty bad.

This was one failing that I was absolutely aware of. I didn't know I was experiencing a lot of sounds, smells, and textures differently than the other children, but I knew full well that all the other kids could identify each other accurately. In the hopes of improving my recognition skills, I spent some serious time looking at people and figuring out what differences distinguished them.

Doing this without the help of an OT or other professional was pretty rough, because I couldn't figure out a way to "get" what faces looked like without spending quite a bit of time staring at other kids.

There are kids who don't like to be stared at who will, if they believe it to be necessary, express this dislike by waiting until recess, then balling up their hands into rounded shapes known in the vernacular as "fists" and using those fists for socially corrective percussive communication. I got punched pretty hard a few times.

Kids who have a sensory discrimination disorder that affects their vision (aka muddled-up sight) can get into a lot of social trouble since people's facial features, facial expressions, and body language are all assumed to be open books for sighted folk. There's no way for another kid to guess that (1) the SPuDster's ability to discern him from other kids may not be super-solid and (b) even if his face is known and recognized, facial expressions may be a mystery to the kid with SPD.

So I worked hard on recognizing faces, and I gradually got somewhat better. I still get confused. At one group meeting, I recently introduced myself to a "new" attendee, and it turned out to be someone I've known as an acquaintance for a few years. But simply practicing facial recognition has helped me much of the time.

So did *Star Trek*. My dad started letting me watch *Star Trek* with him when I was 3, because *Star Trek* is awesome. However, the show was a little over my head sometimes, so I was allowed to ask as many questions as I wanted during commercials.

One recurring question was, "Daddy, why is Captain Kirk's face scrunched up like that?" And the reply was usually, "Well, honey, he's very worried, because his ship is in danger and he loves his ship." Stuff like that.

Even for a little kid with SPD and Asperger's, the contrast between William Shatner's intense acting as Captain Kirk and Leonard Nimoy's relatively phlegmatic portrayal of Spock was enough to make me realize that something was going on with the characters' faces. And because my Dad was watching with me, I received detailed lessons on the meaning of different facial expressions and movements with every episode.

Between consciously trying to figure out how people's faces differ and having my dad as my unknowing instructor in the area of why people's faces get scrunched up, I was way ahead of where a lot of kids with SPD plus Asperger's would have been.

Big Important Note: Like my speech therapy, Star Trek was something I enjoyed. Like music, it was something I really loved. You can get a lot out of kids if you use their natural inclinations and interests as educational tools. It's almost as if engaging a child in a positive way has an actual positive effect or something.

Other Note: *Star Trek* rules. Live long and prosper.

But It's Not All Good

While I did try to report some of my problems with faces to adults on one or two occasions, the results I got were so discouraging that I stopped. There was no teacher in my life who believed it when I protested that I didn't know which child was which or that I had not been able to tell from her face that she had been angry. My protests of visual difficulties were seen as lame excuses, and the assumption was that I was simply trying to weasel out of taking responsibility for my own actions.

Because of that, and because of my fear of looking stupid, I didn't even try to get help for some of my most frustrating sight problems. Who would believe that a child with 20/20 vision simply could not see the red bird on the fence when it was pointed out?

Ah, yes, pointing to things or telling the class where to look to see them. The downside of field trips.

When we were on a field trip to a state park, and the teacher said, "Children, look at that small tree next to the fir tree. That one is a young maple tree," I had no idea what she was talking about.

See, if someone says, "Look at the tree next to X," unless both the tree and X are fairly isolated in my visual field, my chance of finding either one is pretty slim. It's the same with, "Look children, there's a turtle by that bush," and "The bird I'm talking about is right there and it's red, for heaven's sake, what do you mean you can't see it?"

This problem is very hard to explain, possibly because I've never gotten past it. I see just fine, but I often can't locate specific items within a given vista. I can see the forest, and I can see the trees, but I can't pick out a given tree even if it is described clearly and someone is pointing to it.

My dad solved this problem neatly: As a sales engineer, he often had to go into a plant or sewage system or other place chock full of vital equipment and possible issues. Inevitably, someone would point to something and say, "Well, that there is where the main problem is," and my dad would have to go back and forth with the guy or gal as to where and what that there something-or-other actually was. So my dad got a laser pointer.

Carrying a laser pointer means no muss, no fuss, if someone points to a specific item, you can whip out that laser pointer and point specifically to an object so that it's marked with a bright red dot and say, "You mean this?" And if it's the wrong thing, you can always have the other person use the laser pointer and they can identify exactly what they want you to look at. Brilliant.

Of course, the laser pointer doesn't solve all problems. It's great when you're in a manufacturing facility where you're trying to get an idea of how the widget connects to the whatchamacallit next to the whosit, but not so great when you're at the park and someone wants to point out an animal or person. It is not okay to point a laser pointer at strangers, even if they are wearing the exact backpack you yourself are wearing. It is also problematic to use a laser pointer in any place where people walk their dogs. Making random dogs go crazy with the red dot is not a socially appropriate behavior. Even if it is hilarious.

How Bad Could It Get?

Fortunately for me, I can easily keep track of objects like cars around me, whether they are moving or stopping, and thus drive safely. This is not true of all people with SPD that affects their visual processing.

The process that allows us to know that as objects get "larger" in our field of vision they are actually getting closer isn't intuitive to every child. This is another case where your friendly neighborhood behavioral optometrist can be a big help.

For kids with severe visual processing problems, getting lost may be the rule rather than the exception. When one street looks much like another, or when visual information is hard to retrieve, it's easy to wander into the wrong part of the school or neighborhood.

I know an extremely bright young man who is currently doing undergraduate studies. His girlfriend wound up spending untold hours training him to find the places on and near campus that he needed to be. Imagine being a student and not being able to consistently locate the local 24-hour Taco Bell drive thru, even after being there a dozen times!

There are many tasks that we do without ever thinking about what we are actually doing with the vast amount of visual data involved. I can't imagine what it is like for a child with very iffy visual processing to go to the grocery store right after the floor plan has been entirely reorganized. You think you hate it when they change where everything is? Try doing it when you can't pick items out of a visual field without identifying each item separately.

People with sensory discrimination disorder that affects their processing of visual data HATE *Where's Waldo*.

The Most Important Thing

The most important thing my own visual processing problems have affected is, of course, my ability to read comic books.

You may laugh, but I'm dead serious. I tried to read comic books for about a year when I was 11-ish, but found them frustrating and confusing. I simply could not integrate the separate verbal and visual information into one meaningful piece.

That was back in the 1970s, when comic books had come to rely on using pictures not just to illustrate the story but to communicate more than just the text could say. There were times when one or more pages without any text at all were meant to communicate important aspects of stories, characters, and settings.

For those who might care, I was trying to read Marvel, mostly *Fantastic Four* and *Star Wars* comics. Marvel had started using denser and more meaningful visual communication in the late 1960s/early 1970s and never looked back.

I found a book that reprinted a bunch of older Superman comics, and I was thrilled I could read and understand all of it—because the pictures illustrated and recapitulated the text. Since the pictures said pretty much the same thing as the words, I could get by, especially with repeated readings.

Think about what this would mean to a child: If you can't make sense of the visual information in comic books, how much of the visual information are you missing in your day-to-day life? How much social communication is purely visual, and how often do the real intended meanings of words hinge on visual clues like facial expressions and body language?

Thanks to my dad and *Star Trek*, I could make out a lot of that nonverbal communication, but getting the words and visuals to work together was still tough. It took conscious thought for me to pull the two kinds of input together, and that can slow a person's development of social understanding quite a bit.

Came the Dawn

I gave up on comic books for years, frustrated beyond measure. Gradually, comic books became more and more sophisticated, so you could pick up a meaningful dystopian graphic novel or clever dark humor comic if you were so inclined. A great new world of delicious mental, emotional, and psychological stimulation came out of the comic industry, and there I was, fully aware of it and yet bewildered by it.

I bought some comics because they were related to things I loved, but then the Internet clued me into the fact that I missing huge chunks of important stuff every time I read one—and not obscure or minor things, either. I missed not-so-little things: A character could die in one issue, and I'd think he was alive until his death was mentioned in the next issue. Seriously, who dies without narration????

So, I tried. I gave up for a while, I tried, I gave up again.

And then *The Avengers* movie came out, and I realized I desperately needed many, many, many *Thor* comics. About a zillion or so.

And in the wonder of finding reprints of early Thor comics and following stories and characters through years and decades, I started reading enough about comic books to realize much more about what the pictures were saying.

In all of my struggles to read comics over the years, I had never consciously realized that my problem was simply that I couldn't "read" the pictures. My confusion had always had a huge amount of mystery to it; I never had a name for the real problem.

I started reading more slowly and deliberately, looking at the pictures and thinking about what I was seeing. I started piecing together the ways a drawing could affect what the words meant, and what drawings could communicate without words.

It all started coming together. I started being able to really pull meaning out of the visuals, finally really "getting" that there was more to the writing than the words.

And oh-so-weirdly, this all started having an effect on how much meaning I took from visuals in everyday life. I had worked on body language and facial expressions so deliberately, for so many years, that I already had a pretty good grasp of them. It hadn't really occurred to me how much visual information there is in the everyday scenes we all experience.

I Guess This Is Growing Up

This new phase of developing my visual processing is really, really new—note that *The Avengers* only came out about two years ago as of this writing. That's important, and that's the reason I've been babbling about comic books for a couple of pages now.

It turns out that my brain and yours and your child's too are all just waiting for a chance to learn new stuff and develop new skills. I'm doing this stuff in my 40s, and it seems as though the sky is the limit. Less than 2 years of my life have involved this new attack on the comic book problem, and yet I've made huge progress.

This is not at all unique to me. Any neurologist can tell you that "brain plasticity" is a real and important part of everyone's potential. This means that the human brain maintains its ability to develop new connections and new cells right through from childhood to adulthood.

Yes, kids have the ability to change their brains faster than adults, and SPD intervention can have a much greater effect per hour of effort for a 3-year-old than for a 60-year-old. Early intervention is every bit as important as OTs, speech therapists, teachers, and pediatricians tell you, because it takes much less time for that 2-year-old to develop, say, better visual integration than it does for the 60-year-old.

But I wasn't able to overcome all of my personal SPD hurdles as a child. A child may not develop perfect sensory integration by a given deadline. Even after the early years, people can make leaps and bounds in their ability to process, recognize, and make use of the data we take in. There is no due date on success. There is no point at which your child is "done."

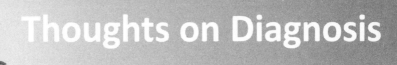

Thoughts on Diagnosis

In this book, I'm not going to just talk about myself and tell stories about myself, I'm also going to brag about myself unabashedly. I know a lot about what SPD is, how it feels to have SPD, and what life is like when you're a SPuDster. I also know a lot about how people with SPD can use their brains to manage their emotions. But I am not an expert on diagnosing and/or treating SPD.

Again: I am not an expert on diagnosing or treating SPD. I'm not even an expert on finding someone competent to diagnose SPD. But I do know enough to give you a few important tips and insights. Enough to be worth putting on paper.

When you suspect your child might have some kind of sensory processing problem, it can be hard to get support. While Temple Grandin, like most adults with autism or Asperger's, thinks it's ridiculous that SPD is not recognized as a real diagnosis, there are a lot of experts and "experts" who simply aren't buying it.

That means it can be hard to get a diagnosis. There are pediatricians who will help and support parents who think SPD might be a possibility, and there are also those who think it's a load of nonsense.

There's a catch-22 going on in the area of research: because SPD is not yet recognized by the medical field as a whole, it can be tough to get funds to do research. It can also be tough to get people interested in doing the necessary research; after all, if you know that you're going to have trouble getting funding, why bother? It takes serious commitment for a researcher to be willing to take as many "no" answers as it takes to get to the point where he or she can actually do the research we need so much.

Lucy Jane Miller, PhD, who I've mentioned previously, is spearheading a lot of really cool research, and I like to give her credit and mad props every time I can. Hi, Dr Miller!!!

Despite all of this, it is possible to get a diagnosis and help for a child with SPD, including both those kids who have SPD as a stand-alone problem and those who have SPD in conjunction with an autism spectrum disorder, learning disability, or other disorder.

Yes, it can be done and it is done every day. The main way it gets done is through stubborn parents who know their kid, know that their kid needs help, and are not prepared to take "no" for an answer.

Parents are the people who call as many pediatricians as it takes to find one who is open to looking at SPD as a possibility. Parents are the people who ask questions of teachers and administrators about the possibility of having their child evaluated by an OT and maybe also a speech-language pathologist through the school district. Parents are usually the first and best advocates children have.

Of course, grandparents (and other relatives or guardians) are often able to advocate for kids with SPD as well as or instead of parents. Never underestimate the power of a motivated senior. Old age is not for wimps!

One resource that can help a parent identify a good direction to go in, a good person to call for info, or a good way to cut through the red tape in the school district is a local or online support group. Finding other parents who have dealt with at least some of what you are going through can help you. The best way to find support groups is through the Internet.

Coincidentally, one good way to find doctors and therapists who are interested in helping children is through the Internet, as well.

This means that if you are seeking a diagnosis or treatment for SPD, the Internet is now your official new best friend.

How I Did It

As I've detailed before, I found out I had SPD only because I was diagnosed with Asperger's Syndrome by a psychologist. So how did I do that?

Well, first I read a lot about Asperger's. I wasn't an expert, but I did enough poking around to be sure that the diagnosis was a likely possibility given the lists of symptoms and tests that I found online and through my public library.

Then I did a bunch of searches on Google. I searched "Asperger's diagnosis," "Asperger's Orange County CA," "autism Asperger's Southern California," "Asperger's learning disability psychologist OC," and a whole lot of other variations.

By using a ton of different related searches, I finally targeted psychologists and doctors who were fairly close to where I lived and who dealt with autism spectrum disorders. I zeroed in on one whose Web site particularly mentioned experience dealing with learning disabilities and ADHD in adults.

Why look at learning disorders and ADHD when I didn't think I had either? Because I wanted someone who knew about these frequently confused but not identical issues so that there would be a clear diagnosis. Getting someone who knew the differences between these similar issues was important to me, as there is a lot of overlap.

I can't tell you this is the best way to get a diagnosis, but it is worth an evening of your time. I do think the Internet is a valuable resource.

Yes, the Internet also harbors quacks and nuts, so do stay alert to what does and doesn't pass the "sniff test." If it metaphorically smells like cow pies, become a seriously skeptical consumer. If someone says that they can tell just via e-mail that your child definitely has SPD and they can cure it through magnetic brain stimulation for just slightly more than your life savings, run, run, run, run, run, run away!

Lest I forget to mention it: There is stellar information at *SPDFoundation. net* and *out-of-sync-child.com.* They are both awesome.

Stick to the Facts

When your child is being evaluated and/or diagnosed, remember the facts. If a doctor, psychologist, OT, or other evaluator says that your child can't write his name, and you know darn well he can write his name, then you need to have a talk with that person.

How well those talks go can tell you a lot about whether that professional is going to be able to give you an accurate idea of what your child does or doesn't have in the way of SPD. If you honestly explain, "Well, he isn't writing his name with that pencil, but he writes it with a crayon at home," and he or she doesn't (at dead minimum) acknowledge your input, then that's a problem.

A professional who is evaluating your child and brushes off your input may not be doing a really meaningful assessment. After all, there are a lot of factors that can affect a child. Being in an unfamiliar space, dealing with people he's never met or barely knows, being asked to do things immediately that he usually does only when he feels like it, or just plain being incredibly rushed by someone who has another eval scheduled in 20 minutes so can we move this along please—all of those things are real issues that can affect your child's diagnosis and therefore what help he does or doesn't get.

This can get pretty extreme. In my case, I was always taught to be at my most polite and nice with authority figures like doctors, which has always translated to me putting my best foot forward if at all possible when I'm in a medical setting. My husband finds this bewildering and kind of hilarious, because he's seen me getting sicker and draggier for days on end, and then, when the doctor walks into the exam room, I perk up and am absolutely pleasant and bright.

In other words, I naturally hide signs of illness when I am around doctors. It has nothing to do with SPD that I know of, it's just a quirk that happens to occasionally cause me to have to go back to the doctor a second time because I forgot to let him know I was sick. I'm working on it.

A much more serious case of unusual behavior during an evaluation happened when a psychologist was assessing my brother Jimmy for autism. Jimmy was about 4 years old and had never met the doctor or been in his office before. After a long evaluation, the doctor let my mom know she could come into the room.

As soon as my mom came in, Jimmy ran over to her, threw his arms around one of her legs, and said, "Mommy, I missed you!"

The doctor was stunned. Stone. Cold. Stunned.

That psychiatrist had been preparing to tell my mom that Jimmy had a very grim prognosis. From his point of view, he had been evaluating a child who was nonresponsive, nonverbal, and completely in his own little autistic world.

Thing is, at that age, Jimmy didn't really recognize people outside of his own family as people. In fact, he wasn't entirely sure of anyone except my mom.

Jimmy had (and has) a lot of autistic traits and a lot of issues that have slowed him down and made it difficult for him to learn to speak fluently, learn to do normal transactions, and to simply interact with the rest of the human race. He still gets "stuck" verbally and has great difficulty reading people. That fairly sophisticated sentence he greeted my mother with was a rarity: At that age, he was still mainly using single words, sometimes supplemented with the simplest of sentences.

My mom had been working incredibly hard, from my brother's first day in the world right up to that evaluation, at encouraging my brother to communicate. She respected his extreme defensiveness against light touch and she worked every possible positive angle she could to get him to play, work, and grow.

With a stranger in a strange room, he couldn't generalize his abilities. He just didn't have what it took to recognize the person evaluating him as a person. He didn't have the ability to interact with the doctor any better than he could interact with, say, a wall. He just couldn't generalize what he knew, but the doctor recognized that Jimmy's response to a family member meant there was a way to draw Jimmy into the world. One moment changed all of the hopes and dreams we might ever have had for Jimmy. (Except, of course, that my mother would never have given up on him ever, regardless of what anybody said.)

Getting your child a correct diagnosis is a tough job. You can do it.

Chapter 9

We've established that there are eight, count them, EIGHT sensory systems, three more than is usually advertised, and there are three major categories of SPD, which break down into smaller categories, most of which can affect any of those eight senses in a number of different ways. This means there are roughly a kabillion different combinations or sub-types of SPD, and that every individual's SPD is different than any other.

So what's a parent to do?

Well, you can work with your child's OT to set goals and track your child's progress. It's important to work together with your OT to make sure both you and he/she know what you're trying to work toward and know what success will look like when it happens.

You can keep in touch with all of the professionals who work with your child and find out what their goals are. After all, if your child has an OT with three important goals, a speech pathologist working toward four important goals, and a teacher who is trying a behavioral approach to get your child to reach another completely different set of two goals, that's a problem. Kids who are super-overloaded by being pushed in many different directions at once get even more overwhelmed than their parents!

But, there are two very very most important things you can do for a child: Encourage him to play, and play with him.

Kids develop through play. Not just motor skills, not just imagination or problem solving, but whole-kid development. Children need play. It's the most serious and important work of childhood.

How important is play? Let me tell you a little story about Fred Rogers. AKA Mister Rogers. The one, the only, the awesomest.

Back when it was first possible for an average person to get a machine that would let them record TV shows (at the time, the VCR), there was a huge legal brouhaha about whether people should be allowed to make their own recordings of TV shows. After all, if people recorded TV shows and movies, that would take money away from the companies that made money by broadcasting them. There was much argle argle argle about it.

Mister Rogers testified before Congress on the side of the VCR manufactures. Let me say that again: Mister Rogers, the most decent, gentle, and incorruptible human being imaginable, went to bat for a huge corporation. Why?

Mister Rogers really wanted parents to be able to record his shows so that children could take advantage of the late afternoon and early evening sunshine to play outside. He also wanted parents to be able to watch his show with their children, which would be impossible if the show aired before parents got home from work.

Mister freakin' Rogers felt play was *that* important. Note that he also wanted parents and kids to watch his show *together*.

Two of the greatest gifts you can give your child are *play* and *time*.

I remember the K-12 world as if it were a vast swamp of muck that I had to trudge through, head down, slogging toward heaven knows what goal. When I think about that, I think about how much childhood sucked and how glad I am that I'm never going back.

When I think about playing and being with my parents, I remember going out for a catch with my dad after dinner in the spring, shading my eyes against the lowering sun. I remember my mom being willing to be just plain silly with me and to slog through the mess in my room with me. I felt like I could do anything if my mom was on my side.

I didn't learn American history because I was taught it at school, I learned it because my parents took us to Colonial Williamsburg and because they played the original cast album of *1776* about a zillion times. I learned to love Sherlock Holmes because they were super-excited when they bought the annotated version of the complete stories and even fought a little over who had possession of a given volume of it at a given time.

My parents taught me a great deal through *fun*. They shared what they loved with their children and gave their time to their children.

Not all parents have the luxury of giving their children tons of time or trips to history sites and museums. But whenever you can spare time or energy just for play, just for sharing something fun or interesting or silly, it matters.

There's a new public service campaign out that is working hard to get parents to spend 15 minutes a day reading to their children. If you can do it, do it. Get fun books at the public library, as well as "educational" ones, because the time and energy and connection will be better if your kids can enjoy and be happy.

Your kids will have better lives if they learn to play. Your kids will have better lives if they have YOU.

Not Going Soft

Much as I know the warm fuzzy stuff is based in hard facts and reality, there is another aspect to being a parent. You have to be mean.

No, I don't mean you have to forbid your child happiness or ruin their lives by never letting them do the fun things the other kids do, but as a parent, you sure do have to prevent them from molding themselves to the couch. Part of the reason time with a parent is great is that parents are not "friends" with their kids, but something more. And that means you have to be tough as nails and totally heartless.

Trust me, it takes a will of iron to tell a 4-year-old with autism that he is only allowed to watch Disney's Mary Poppins once per day. It takes a heart of stone to limit an 11-year-old with Asperger's and SPD to only two hours a day of television. It can take the grim determination of a person climbing Mount Everest to refuse to allow either of those children their God-given right to have their own TV in their rooms.

Oh, the weeping and wailing that went on when my parents chose play over electronics and made us learn to entertain ourselves or at least not limit ourselves to only one mode of entertainment all day non-stop.

This is all part of something you will hear a lot as a parent (or teacher) of a child with SPD. It's called a "good sensory diet." It's a big deal.

What's a Sensory Diet?

If you are dealing with any professional in the field of SPD, if you read books about or even just Google SPD, you will soon run across the term "sensory diet." In fact, there will be a lot of people telling you that your child needs a better sensory diet and that you need to implement this throughout the day. So what gives?

Humans have a tendency to adore being inert and entertained—especially people with over-responsivity, dyspraxia, or any of those other fun sensory problems that make it hard to play actively in an "age-appropriate" way. If you have a tendency to flail and panic during tetherball, if you see using the teeter-totter as a blood sport, or if you just get overwhelmed by the sights and smells of the everyday world, there is a natural tendency to avoid the outdoors and pretty much any kind of unfamiliar input.

Kids who are under-responsive, the ones who need a marching band in their room to get them sufficiently awakened to be able to get dressed, also tend to spend little time digging into new surroundings. They may go to the park or hang out in the backyard, but if they don't have some impetus to start with, their surroundings may not have enough oomph to get them engaged.

Last, we have the kids who are sensory craving. If a kid tends to run everywhere, knock into everyone and everything, and lick stuff in situations where licking stuff is pretty much not a good social move, then parents, teachers, and just about anybody trying to corral the kid will be pretty nervous about taking that kid into novel situations. If a kid has a tendency to put his face directly in the sand on a sand table at school, or to use finger paint to paint any and all surfaces at home, there is an understandable and quite sane desire not to take this kid to a place where he may decide to use mud in a variety of creative and possibly actionable ways.

So, what does this mean for the whole sensory diet thing? Well, the term sensory diet actually means getting a human to experience different kinds of sensory environments and things.

The idea is that when a kid is having trouble because his brain is not connecting up well with his input processes, like seeing, touching, and smelling, then he needs to exercise those input processes. Like if you have poor upper body strength, you might want to do stuff that makes your upper body muscles active in order to start building up those special muscles which give you good enough posture to spend 3 hours solid playing Candy Crush Saga without getting (much of) a stiff neck.

Just as you can make your body stronger through exercise, you can build up your sensory processing apparatus through exercising your senses. Cool, huh?

This means that kids with SPD often need to get out of their everyday ruts. Trips to that strange place we call "outside" are frequently in order. Using toys with different textures and weights means input for the tactile sense and the muscle sense. Eating (or learning to tolerate being in the same room as) foods with differing textures or tastes is a good thing too.

Now, one caution: You still need to do that vital parent thing of knowing when to back off or bail out. If you take your over-responsive kid to the park and there are about a million kids there already, you are going to have to use your own judgment as to whether this is a day that's going to rock or a day when just 5 minutes of trying to use the same jungle gym as 50 other kids is going to cause a giant hairy cat-fit.

And yes, I do realize that sometimes you don't find out that your approach is going to cause a giant hairy cat-fit until it actually happens. And sometimes you've got a kid who insists that she wants to swing on the swings despite the crowding, and 5 minutes later you have to scrape her off the asphalt because the chaos of every swing being occupied by a different kid who is swinging at a different speed and rhythm than she is has caused her fight-flight-freeze instinct to go into overdrive.

I hated it when there were too many kids swinging. I still don't like it when people go in and out of my peripheral vision constantly, like they are hovering. How the heck my brain is NOT going to see that as a sign that they are time-traveling Nazi terrorists who have been sent to kidnap me to use my brain in unholy experiments, I don't know.

So having a good sensory diet means adding new experiences and activities into your child's life even if it means nudging him into unfamiliar territory.

A Caveat

Developing and improving sensory processing is a lot like developing any skill that involves coordinating your brain and nervous system with the rest of the body. This means going with activities that are not too far from what the child can already do. It's called "scaling" (or, sometimes, "scaffolding"), and it's a vital concept.

Suppose you knew a fellow who has been in a bad accident, and he was currently unable to walk, but the doctors said he'd be able to walk and even run again in time with therapy. What if the physical therapist told him, on his first visit, that he had to get ready for a 5K that weekend?

You'd think the physical therapist was nuts, right? You don't go from "not able to walk" to running a race in a few days. You don't help someone develop a tough skill like "relearning how to walk" by just telling him to get up and go jogging already!

The same thing applies to kids with SPD (and humans in general). If your kid can't tolerate noise and you take her to a crowded place with no earmuffs or earplugs and just expect her to "dig deep," what you will get is a basket case. The kid who struggles to get a bat anywhere near a ball needs a lot of help developing strength and coordination before he can start specifically learning to play baseball with any level of functionality.

Scaffolding (scaling) means you build a child up bit by bit. You don't build a 10-story building without building a scaffold that allows the workers to reach what they need to build, and you don't build a kid without giving him the support he needs to get where he is going bit by bit.

End of lecture. Beginning of next lecture.

Perfection Is Not an Option

This is not about coming up with a 5-year plan for a carefully scaled buildup of sensory input. It's not about turning your life even more upside down to fit in dozens of new sensory experiences each week. It's about playing some, going to the park some, and generally getting your kid to do something fun that's just a teeny bit outside of his usual sphere.

For my mom, this meant having basic toys was important. As far as she was concerned, we needed toys that didn't do a darned thing. Dolls weren't supposed to walk or talk on their own, because we were supposed to do the talking and walking for them. Building toys were important because they required thought and patience. Also, building a tower as high as possible and then knocking it down is great fun—fun is good. Enjoying yourself is an important part of play, and un-smart toys are actually fun!

If a child is really used to toys that do the playing for him, he may not immediately fully embrace toys that require him to do the actual physical and imaginative work; that is to say, he may be really, really upset about restrictions on computer and video time and deeply believe that wooden blocks are Satan's curbstones. It can be a tough transition, but play is the serious work of childhood. Play is how the nervous system grows, how our understanding of cause-and-effect develops, and how we learn to use our brains and creativity.

Remember, play is just as important as academic skills and factual knowledge. It's great when a child is advancing in school and in skills like reading and math, but if the child is spending too much valuable free playing time on trying to get ahead, he can miss out in many ways. You can learn algebra at age 17 or 28 just as well as you can at 13, but childhood play is magic.

Batteries Not Included

My mom spent some serious time reading up on child development, so she knew very well the importance of play. When other kids' parents bragged about how their children learned to read at 3 (or 2, or whatever) by using such-and-such a system, she would smile blandly and wait for a more interesting topic to opine on. She knew that many of those preschoolers were missing out on valuable and, in fact, irreplaceable developmental activities, but she wasn't going to blast anyone—and she wasn't going to let anyone cause her to feel inferior because her kids weren't taking SAT prep classes at 5.

This also meant my mom would seldom, if ever, buy replacement batteries for battery-powered toys. If you wanted the little dog to jump and bark, instead of getting new batteries to replace the ones that came with the toy, you had to make the little dog jump and bark yourself.

(The first set of batteries usually came with the toy—not because the manufacturer included them, but because our grandparents and other relatives knew full well that otherwise, there wouldn't be batteries for those toys.)

My grandma (my mother's mother) understood play as well. One year she knew I really wanted a nice doll, so she went out to get one, but she couldn't find one that was good enough. Why? Because at store after store, it was impossible to find a doll that *didn't do anything*. There were dolls that cried, crawled, ate, and otherwise entertained, but finding a doll that did nothing seemed impossible.

Fortunately for me, Grandma was not a woman to compromise easily. She kept looking until she found a doll that did absolutely nothing but be a doll. It is the one doll I still have. Long after RC car-riding Baby-Go-Bye-Bye and Real-Hair-Growing Crissy and Talking Mrs Beasley (it was a 1970s thing, long story) have fallen by the wayside or been forgotten, lost, or donated, I still have my Ginnie Baby doll. She still does everything she did the day I got her, which means her hair never did grow back, but she is still with me.

There were other toys that did nothing and were awesome. My uncle's pristine old metal toy trucks (with plenty of small detachable parts, guaranteed to pinch your fingers) were great, as were building toys of any kind. We had Giant Tinkertoys, which were big enough to build a playhouse you could use as a playhouse. We had trikes and then bikes and a wagon to share.

My sister and I did just fine with predominantly plain old toys. I'm not saying cool electronic stuff is bad—heck, video games are incredibly great for developing fine-motor skills, and there are about a zillion educational apps and just plain fun apps to play with out there. But having a good sensory diet means that not all toys do your imagining and your playing for you.

Better Than Advertised

Sometimes even I, who was not all that thrilled by some of my mom's ideas about toys, had to admit she was a genius who came up with the most awesome stuff ever. We got some really good stuff that worked way better than the official toys out there.

One Christmas the top item on my sister's list was an Easy-Bake Oven. For those of you not familiar with the Easy-Bake Oven, it looks like a very small oven and allows children to bake teeny-tiny cakes and cookies via the heat of an incandescent light bulb. It is definitely one of those toys that requires adult supervision, because by definition, it has to get hot enough to bake stuff.

My mom was not big on the Easy-Bake Oven idea. The toy baked tiny cakes from tiny mixes that cost way too close to what an actual cake mix cost, and it required a parent to supervise constantly. So she was being asked to put her day on hold while her kid or kids mixed a powder with water and heated it with a light bulb. Geesh.

What was more, it was a hideously inefficient way to learn to make a cake. It didn't teach any actual cooking or baking skills, as it didn't require an egg to be cracked or dry ingredients to be measured.

So my mom did not get my sister the much-desired Easy Bake Over. Instead, she got one of the best gifts anyone ever got.

On Christmas morning, my sister unwrapped a huge box, and inside it she found a mixing bowl, measuring cups, measuring spoons, cake mixes, and pretty much all the other little things she would need to actually bake stuff.

I was insane with jealousy. If I had known that insisting on an Easy-Bake Oven would produce such amazing results, I would have been whining for one every day of the year.

My mom figured that being as she would have to supervise the whole process anyway, my sister might as well learn to actually bake a cake. There were a ton of pluses, not the least of which was that when there was no actual baking going on, my sister had cool stuff like measuring cups and bowls to play with.

Getting to play with measuring cups and spatulas and all that good stuff is a super addition to a sensory diet. Measuring water, mud, or rocks is always fun, and it's a great way to get good and dirty. (Or, if your child is horrified by dirt, measuring dried beans is good and not icky.) Measuring, scooping, and mixing make up one of those great games where the play itself is insanely fun and builds a healthy brain at the same time. Neural connections that support sensory processing development? You are up to your elbows in all of those when you've got your own kitchen utensils.

Even better, it's cheap, so it's truly fun. When Mom or Dad picks up a bunch of measuring spoons and mixing bowls from the dollar store, a kid can play as roughly as he wants. It really doesn't matter if you break a dollar's worth of spatulas, and that means the kid who grips things too hard and is struggling to learn not to break stuff can have fun without fearing the Wrath of Mom.

I'm pretty sure my mom saved money on the deal. She sure would now: Easy Bake Ovens cost about $60 a pop. How much would a trip to the dollar store for measuring cups and bowls cost?

What's more, those great kitchen-type toys can be used in real-life cooking lessons. We had something called Betty Crocker's Cookbook for Boys and Girls, and we learned to cook starting with the incredibly simple. We also "helped" Mom in the kitchen frequently.

I should hasten to add that I know there are only so many times Mom and Dad can involve a child (with or without SPD) in the cooking process. When you are just learning what your child's problems and limits are, it can be super-hard to have him in the kitchen because you can't accurately gauge what he's likely to be able to do without too much chaos erupting. If he's a sensory craver, it may be better to encourage him to help with chores that do not involve edibles or the potential to coat the entire kitchen in a thin layer of vegetable oil.

We will not discuss here the effort and time it took my mom to teach me how to correctly break (and eventually separate) eggs. I will only say that I did learn to do so before I moved out of the house, and that was soon enough.

Play and "Heavy Work"

There's another term that comes up often in books and discussions about SPD: "heavy work." Heavy work means work that involves solid physical effort to reach a clear goal, such as lifting something that is heavy enough that you can feel it a bit. Heavy work, like play, can be magic.

The sensory-craving kid who goes every which way all the time and gets more wound up the more she goes? She's likely to thrive on heavy work. The over-responsive kid who is super-touchy and flinches most of the day may also find relief and a pathway to emotional calm through doing adequate heavy work. The under-responsive kid? You guessed it. Heavy work can get the brain and body back on speaking terms pretty darn quick.

Heavy work can be really simple, like filling pails with water from the faucet to help fill up the kiddie pool, or carrying books, or moving furniture out of the way for a game. In fact, simple is often good; the straightforward purposefulness of heavy work seems to be part of what makes it work; at least, that's a part of it for me.

And heavy work isn't just for kids. One thing that I have to do to stay sane and in touch with my muscles is (ahem) "weight training." Sure, I use teensy dumbbells—no more than 10 pounds—but doing enough sets of curls to make my tiny muscles hit tilt does amazing things for my brain. Regular bouts of moderately strenuous exercise are one of my most important tools to ward off the specters of depression and anxiety (common in adults who grew up with undiagnosed SPD).

Heavy work does have to be right for the child. The energy and strength of each person is different, and what would calm and even energize one kid might just wipe out another.

In my case, as I said, I'm gradually working my way up to 10-pound weights, in the full knowledge that I knew people in grade school who would have, even when they were kids, found my little teeny dumbbells and exhausting four sets of 12 reps to be oh-so-cute. I'm not super-strong, but I'm stronger than I would be without the effort. And I can actually feel where my body is!

More Sensory Diet Tips, Courtesy of My Mom

I must say, my mom was pretty fiendish when it came to promoting motor skills with day-to-day activities. She was clever about getting us to do heavy work more or less of our own free will, too. Then again, some of it was just necessary.

When my parents, my sister, and I all moved in to my parents' current house, the yard was a bit lacking. Specifically, the builder had used dirt cheap filler "earth" to make up for the lack of same in our front yard, and thus, we had a problem: The ground was filled with so many rocks that growing a lawn, never mind a garden, was going to be impossible.

So, my parents set to work. They spent a lot of time over a lot of weekends digging the stones out of the yard and tossing them into the creek at the end of the backyard. It was extremely hard work, and they had a 7-year-old and a 3-year-old to watch while they did it. Three guesses how they managed that.

Yep, my sister and I were out there digging rocks with them. We weren't expected to do very much, but outfitting us with small digging spades meant we were there and active.

If I recall correctly, my sister was working with a toy beach bucket and sand spade. I'm pretty sure she didn't dig up all that many big rocks, but she found small ones to put in her bucket and then dump them into the wheelbarrow with the rest. Also, she sat down a lot. And I think she tried to eat the spade a couple of times. Hey, she was barely 3.

No matter! We were out there and digging! And no matter how poorly muscled I was, no matter how aggressively mediocre my motor skills were, I wanted to dig out the biggest rocks I could handle and be a big help, because I had an ego the size of Cleveland.

Thing is, if I had been involved in a physical activity like this with other children my age, I would have given up pretty darn quick. I'm certain that other kids my age could have dug faster and lifted heavier rocks, but without them around to make me feel bad, I tried super-hard.

Let me point this out again: With no other kids "competing" with me, I tried my hardest. When a kid is way behind in any area of development, they need the support and encouragement that goes with working for a personal best, not competing with kids who are miles ahead of them in sensory integration.

So I dug rocks, and I enjoyed it. I didn't work continuously, but man, I did work. At one point, I found what I realized must be the biggest rock ever. Digging at it, I found myself hitting a long, long edge that simply must have been one side of one mammoth rock.

When I couldn't uncover it myself, I got my dad, and he started digging too. We dug and dug and eventually started to get the outline of the thing, uncovering enough to see clearly that … it was the hull of a car.

Yes, buried somewhere in my parents' lawn to this day is the hull of an unidentified vehicle. There was just no way to dig the whole thing up.

Trust me, digging up a car was the most awesome thing EVER for me as a 7-year-old. How can you top that?

So, yes, Mom made her children dig rocks in the summer heat. And it was great. It sure as heck wasn't the last time we'd work.

THE WORLD'S BEST SANDBOX

My parents were cool enough to build the WORLD'S BEST SANDBOX. It was a mammoth thing, built first in my dad's workshop and then in place in the backyard. It was gigantic, about 8 feet on a side and far deeper than the average sandbox as well. It ruled!

Yes, you can get a kid to play in the sand more often if he has a sandbox that is better than any other sandbox that has ever been created in the entire history of sandboxes. It probably would not have worked for kids who found sandboxes to be a horrifying sensory experience, but once a kid can handle the sandbox, a really, really big sandbox is the best kind. Have I said sandbox enough yet?

We had to work for it, though. It wasn't just a matter of providing a great place for play that promoted sensory integration and motor skills, it was also about the sand.

Biggest and best sandboxes require an enormous amount of sand. Usually, people buy sand for sandboxes in sacks at the home and gardening store, but my mom calculated the amount of sand needed and realized it would be far cheaper to simply order sand by a truckload.

A real dump truck then came to our house and dumped a huge amount of sand on the part of driveway closest to the sandbox. A real dumptruck! How could anything be cooler?

Well, it got a little less cool right after that. The sand had to be transported to the sandbox, and my mom made it absolutely crystal clear that there were limits to how many hours of hauling sand she and Dad were going to do. We had to help.

Once again, the sand spades and beach buckets came out. My sister and I were quickly involved in the process of hauling sand from the driveway to the new sandbox, bucket by bucket.

When our parents weren't using the wheelbarrow, we also used our buckets to put as much sand in the wheelbarrow as I could manage. There were some immediately practical lessons in how full a wheelbarrow I could handle. Sand everywhere.

Again, if other kids had been around, I probably would have given up in humiliation over how little sand I could actually manage to tote. But it was just me and my sister. We worked our butts off.

Normal parents don't necessarily do stuff like this. It would have made perfect sense for my parents to do the heavy work themselves, but then we would have learned that we were too little and weak to do it. We also wouldn't have had nearly so much pride in our amazing sandbox. It worked for us physically and emotionally.

By the way, if you put an awesome sandbox in your backyard, please remember that an awesome sandbox needs an equally awesome cover. Neighborhood cats love an awesome sandbox too, and cat poop is simply not part of a good sensory diet.

Our Sluggish Selves and Sensory Diets

It took more than cool toys and unpaid child labor for my mom to get me going. While this certainly doesn't apply to everyone on earth, most—if not all—people who are reading up on SPD are living in a place, time, and segment of society in which most adults and most kids can very easily become sedentary in their habits. I was no exception.

It is awfully easy to have the exact opposite of a good sensory diet these days. Tactile input can be limited to the smooth feeling of a keyboard, remote, or touchscreen, and visual input can be bounded by the edges of an LCD or LED screen.

Mind you, it wasn't this way when I was a kid. When I was a kid, if you wanted to change the TV channel, you had to walk over to the television and turn an actual dial—none of this pushing buttons while sitting down stuff!

As you might guess from the above paragraph, I really do think that the belief in an idealized past in which anyone could easily attain good muscle tone, a healthy weight, and perfect sensory functioning through everyday activities is basically a fairy tale. Humans have spent untold generations complaining about how kids today are practically inert because they spend all of their time reading penny dreadful, listening to phonographs, glued to the radio, reading comic books, watching TV, playing video games and/or surfing the internet.

Allegedly there were people who thought that the invention of writing would make kids stupid and lazy. If you could just write stuff down instead of memorizing it, well, there goes civilization!

And yes, I know that there are a lot of people who deeply believe that while all previous generations were wrong to blame the printing press, the iron horse, radio, movies, television and so forth for a non-existent disastrous deterioration in kids, we mature adults of this time and place are right that videogames and YouTube are going to lead to the fall of civilization. I would like to posit the idea that possibly they are wrong. This fault is not in our stars, but in our selves. Including me.

It's not the computer or the TV. It's how humans react to pain. When most if not all unexpected sensory input is painful, it is easy and natural to want to shut out those painful inputs and avoid the unexpected.

That's what most of the things we blame for our kids' (and our own) problems have in common: They are ways to shut out painful experiences and feed highly specific and predictable sensory input into our brains. Books, radio, comic books, TV, video games—they all fulfill the same need, and all can be overused.

Except for comic books. You can never have too many comic books.

A video game may be loud and may involve hostile forces suddenly attacking you, but it is still something you chose when and how to play. You can put in earbuds and shut out all sound but the game play—and turn that sound up or down to suit you. "Bad guys" that you get to shoot when they startle you are way easier to deal with than regular people who freak you out by touching you and then scold you if you react badly.

It's not just kids who startle easily or want to shut out the world that seek out familiar, soothing, and controllable input, however. It's also the under-responsive kid who feels dumb, the over-responsive kid who is an anxious bundle of nerves, and the sensory craving kid who is perceived as a troublemaker and wants to feel like a hero, instead.

All of these kids will find escapist entertainment that provides controlled sensory input, from books to virtual reality, to be a great way to get away from their very real stress and strain. Instantly you can go from being a "problem child" to being the savior of the universe. You can go from being the limp kid with the postural disorder to being a big strong hero. Open a book, pop in a video game, and there you are. Video games just have the advantage of being more having points and levels. You know you always want to reach the next level!

This means that there are a lot of kids with SPD who will seek out the most sedentary indoor activities that our sedentary species can create. You can blame technology for kids having totally lame sensory diets these days, but the biggest problem is that we as humans want to avoid pain. It's a dysfunctional response to a very real problem, and it takes work on the part of parents and other adults to push kids toward solutions that work better in the long run.

So what's a parent to do? How do you compete with all of the electronic toys and indoor activities that are out there?

You don't compete. You limit them and you get your child involved in other activities—including being genuinely bored. You as a parent get to be the mean person who won't let your kids keep gaming devices in their rooms and who limits the time they get to spend using electronics to pump entertainment directly into their brains.

Under these circumstances, kids may complain that they are bored if they think that will get them back that game or toy or whatever it was. They generally figure if they whine enough about being bored, you'll let them play *Undead City of Death Monsters and Beheading Stuff* just to get them to shut up. But instead, when they whine about being bored, you make them go outside to play. Or they can choose between stopping their whining or being stuck in the most boring room in the house for 15 minutes. Whatever works.

You don't create a great sensory diet by returning to simpler times before the coming of the many electronic entertainment devices. You create a great sensory diet by placing limits on those devices so that your child can learn to limit himself.

That's key, by the way. If you gave your kid infinite access to any junk food he wanted, he would learn to eat badly. If you insist that your child eat only absolutely perfectly "right" foods and forbid treats, the second he gets his hands on a Hershey bar, he will curse your name and seek "illicit" food whenever he can get it.

If you give your child infinite access or no access to the Angry Birds, Hulu, or the Internet in general he may not learn to spend time on anything else. But if you cut him off completely from those things, not only are you taking good stuff away from him, you are also leaving him without the skills to take it or leave it.

Television can be a source of awesome knowledge, challenging content, or just plain goofy fun. Video games can improve fine-motor coordination and teamwork skills. The Internet can teach a lot, especially about the social world. All of the things that would add up to a lousy sensory diet on their own can instead have a valuable place in life.

So, in a world of extremely cool and potentially habit-forming electronics, how does a parent set boundaries and make sure a child's sensory diet isn't entirely pixel-based? I've said it needs doing, but how to implement it?

First of all, if it ain't a necessity, parents need to be in charge of it. My blessed, sweet, adorable mother controlled snacks, desserts, and television with a (figurative) fist of iron—and there was no velvet glove involved. The woman is adorable—she makes Snuggles the fabric softener bear look like Penn Jillette (yes, that's a geek shout out, from *Mystery Science Theater 3000* yet)—yet if I snuck in one extra half-hour of TV she came down on me like a ton of bricks. By which I mean that she would heavily dock my TV time and take away my afternoon milk and cookies so fast it would make my head swim.

The reason she needed to control all non-necessities was that she could then teach me to control them. And that's key not just to starting a good sensory diet, but also to giving a child the skills to seek out and maintain that sensory diet in adulthood.

Here is one story that will show you how this was/is done. It was the BIGGEST CRISIS OF MY CHILDHOOD (that week). It was the Great Television Debacle.

The Great Television Debacle

I am going to look very very old very very quickly by telling you that there were essentially no computers or video games for my mom to control when I was a kid. Oh, sure, our TI-99 had two game cartridges—*MunchMan* and *Alien Attack*, if I recall correctly—but the joysticks were so flimsy that any serious game play ended in broken bits of plastic and general frustration. It was effectively self-limiting.

But oh, baby, we did have television. In a world of unpleasant, scary, and unpredictable sensory input, one thing was for sure: *The Addams Family* was on channel 17 at 1:00 PM, and I would be sure to tune in.

During the summer, the way I made sure to be there for my favorite programs was to start watching around 8 o'clock in the morning, and keep watching all day. (This was, of course, in the summer. During the school year, I didn't get to start watching TV until the late afternoon, which was sheer torture.) I knew every station's schedule by heart, which was pretty easy because there weren't very many stations available at the time.

Despite the meager offerings of broadcast TV, I managed to stay glued to the set. I cannot begin to tell you how many times I watched the Brady Bunch go to Hawaii and meet Vincent Price. I cannot begin to tell you how well I learned to adjust the rabbit ears and metal hoop antennas. (You kids get off my lawn!)

My mom had read enough about child development to know that this was not a good thing. She was dealing with a cranky child who was isolated and pale. She didn't need a book on SPD to figure out that she needed to light a fire under my butt.

As you no doubt know from many TV shows and movies about cops, things can be done one of two ways: the easy way or the hard way. My mom offered me the easy way for a while: She urged me to watch less TV and came up with alternative activity suggestions. She mentioned this strange place called "outside" and the possibility of listening to music on the radio I had in my room and doing something called "dancing" to fill some time.

The easy way did not pan out. I was not buying it a bit: it sounded very much like it would interfere with my ability to PUMP TELEVISION DIRECTLY INTO MY BRAIN ALL DAY. I was so very not into it.

You know what happens if you don't do it the easy way. You have to do it the hard way. I didn't know what the hard way entailed, but my mom did, and she thought about it carefully, creating a bulletproof plan that she reworked at length with my dad to make sure there were no loopholes and they were both on board with all of it. United front and all that.

She unveiled her fiendish plan at dinner one night. I and my sister (who watched a moderate amount of TV—she was just collateral damage) were told that from that moment on, we were on a TV allowance. We each got a total of 14 hours of tube time a week, to be used as we saw fit, but only for that week. No saving up from week to week, no rollover minutes, and no sneaking any extra in.

Fourteen hours a week is a lot of TV time. Temple Grandin's mom only gave her an hour a day, and look how much better she turned out than I did.

My mom went with the more generous 14 hours a week because she knew I watched shows that had a whole lot of redeeming social importance or that inspired me to research new topics at the library. She didn't want me to give up nourishing stuff just because junk food was limited. (See, I brought that analogy around again. It's just like actual literature.)

Here's the thing: Suddenly I had to work within boundaries and make decisions. Instead of just banning TV, my mom had found a way to make me pick and choose, to figure out what was important and what was worth skipping. This is a huge and important life skill for all humans, and it applies in a lot of situations: time management, household budgeting, and cleaning out closets, to name a few.

My mom killed a flock of birds with a single stone. The most important thing was that she forced me to get bored. A bored child is more likely to take up "nonpreferred tasks," meaning that a kid who loves TV but is willing to do something else like finger-paint or play in the sandbox may well wind up doing that good sensory stuff simply because it's such an improvement over doing nothing.

It also meant that she had an easier time making me participate in activities that broadened my sensory horizons. I was more likely to take her up on a suggestion of playing outside if the alternative of the boob tube was not available.

As I've mentioned, I have a brother way younger than I am. When he started being the one who needed limits, my mom had to come up with new approaches and seek advice from his OT and teachers for ways to make sure he didn't have wind up spending too much time in the light of the LCD screen.

For my brother, the first limiting rule was, "You can only watch *Mary Poppins* once a day." Hey, when you have a young kid with autism, that's actually a realistic restriction that takes effort to enforce. Your mileage may vary.

As Jimmy got older, he got something I thought was brilliant: charts on the fridge depicting how much time he did (and didn't) get for various activities. Computer time was broken down into chunks of 15 minutes, and he could lose those if he failed to do chores, and he could earn more by doing specific activities.

Again, this serves more than one purpose. The most important one, at least as far as this book is concerned, was making sure Jimmy didn't spend too much time on something that limited his sensory diet, but he also learned that you only have so much of things (budgeting) and that if you want more than you have, you have to earn it (money skills).

And there were limits on what he could earn—there was no way to save up for a week of endless computer games, but there were plenty of ways to snag an extra few minutes for today.

I can't tell you how much computer time, game time, or TV time is appropriate for your child. Different ages, different activities, and different purposes make a difference. Obviously, using the computer for schoolwork is different than just playing around.

Note that you can only actually control this sort of thing when you can see what your kid is doing. Having a gaming console in his bedroom will thoroughly undermine this kind of plan.

More importantly, a gaming console in his bedroom means you have no way of knowing what he's actually playing, whom he's teaming up with via the Internet, or whom else he may be communicating with. That's a problem.

Yes, I'm aware that the social aspects of gaming aren't strictly a sensory thing, but kids with SPD often wind up falling behind on social skills. Working to improve their sensory functioning will give them a chance to catch up over time, but that doesn't mean they can afford to learn social skills from random online gamers. There are plenty of great people who are into gaming, but the nasty and inappropriate people are often louder.

Your kid will likely find all of this at best annoying and at worst horrifically mean. For some reason kids are not always happy about limited computer time, only using the computer in public areas of the house, and having a parent and/or guardian frequently looking over his shoulder.

You can't effectively limit gaming/computer/TV time unless you can actually see what your kid is doing. If you aren't able to effectively limit and oversee that time, his sensory diet will suffer. A lot.

I know that this sucks. It is absolutely unfair that parenting takes so much work and energy. The problem is that if you try to be lenient too much of the time, you can easily wind up paying dearly for it later. And your kid will pay for it too.

Kids with SPD need all the help they can get to become more mature in sensory abilities, social abilities, and emotional self-regulation. If you monitor and restrict their time with electronics, you will give them a big, big boost in all of those areas.

Deciding over time what is age appropriate, gradually giving your child more say over what she reads, plays, and posts online, those are tough jobs too. There is no easy way out.

Several of the members of my "blue ribbon parenting panel" (parents who have input on and veto power over my parenting advice and information) have told me over and over again, "If you are comfortable and relaxed about how parenting is going, you're probably doing it wrong." I wish I could argue with that.

Not Just an Excuse

You can readily see from the information given in previous chapters that my mother was not exactly "soft" on her kids. She created rules, boundaries, and activities that made all of us get active and helped us grow through play.

All of that is super-great, but at the same time, the fact is that the adults around me did not understand my very real limitations and difficulties. Mom was great at creating activities and rules to keep me off the sofa, but the adults around me did not realize how often they were ignoring or missing real problems.

This is *not* about holding a pity party for me. Compared to most humans throughout all of history, I have *always* lived pretty well. I've always had access to TV, movies, a stereo, and a fairly regular supply of chocolate. Today, I have a sweet life; my actual job is writer/speaker, I have a bachelor's degree in computer science (which is a seriously sweet field of study) I'm happily married, and blah, blah, blah, awesome, awesome, awesome. You get the idea. Childhood sucked, but I got out alive.

Yet being constantly doubted and misunderstood is hard on a human being, and growing up with those things as constants is super-painful. We need to use reasoning to understand kids with SPD, because children thrive and succeed when they get understanding and support in addition to boundaries and limitations.

Excuses and Reason

One thing SPD has in common with autism spectrum disorders, ADHD, and learning disabilities is that people who haven't lived with it often label it as "just an excuse." The assumption is that SPD is a way for problem children or problem parents to get away with bad behavior, laziness, stubbornness, and even simple incompetence on a regular basis.

Thing is, all of those things happen sometimes in kids with SPD. Kids with SPD do have the capacity to be disobedient, to procrastinate, or to just be difficult to deal with. Humans are like that sometimes.

But when a diagnosis of SPD is either given or suspected, there are some real problematic behaviors that come up in the adults around the child involved. Some adults are just thick, some don't have the time or background to look behind the behaviors, and some are overwhelmed with multiple children pulling them in a seemingly infinite number of directions. That last can occur with a teacher in a classroom, a parent with two or more kids (seriously, two kids can go in like 20 directions at once), or a medical professional that has all of 11 minutes to evaluate each child.

One common excuse for pooh-poohing the possibility of an SPD diagnosis is simple: Mom or Dad has seen little Jimmy-Beth do a great job of reading, memorization, conquering a physical hurdle like a tall jungle gym, or any of a thousand childhood accomplishments. So said Parent points out: "She doesn't have this sensory thing, she can do just fine when she wants to!" Or, better yet, "She's just stubborn—she could do it if she really wanted to."

So on the one hand you've got a child who can pay infinite attention to a fish tank, to the extent of knowing every fish by species and name, but when he's in class, he seems to not see or hear much of what happens and can't sit still 90% of the time. It seems obvious enough that if he can watch a fish tank for an hour solid, he can pay attention to the teacher.

Except. Except those are different situations at different times. Watching fish in a tank can mean shutting everything else out but the visual sense. There is no need for any other sense to be operating at all, and there is no chance the fish will send him to the principal's office if he spaces out and misses 5 minutes.

Not only that, but EVERYBODY learns better when a subject interests them. EVERYBODY has an easier time focusing and paying attention to something they love or find to be flat-out awesome. It's part of being human: It is just plain harder to focus when the topic isn't innately rewarding to you as an individual.

We all know lots of examples of this happening. There is the guy/gal who can't hear their spouse when the baseball game is on. The friend who takes a month to get comfortable with the new system at work, who can pick up a totally unfamiliar video game and master it in days or even hours. The woman who is a brilliant engineer but who can't remember birthdays or appointments. The teen who can practice guitar for hours on end but who struggles to focus for even a half-hour on history homework.

I know a guy, a mentally healthy, fairly intelligent, and more or less "normal" kind of guy, who I'm pretty sure could walk on an unset broken leg if it meant getting to see Brian Wilson perform. He would be right there in line for tickets, while the people around him said, "Dude, maybe you should get that protruding bone looked at!"

(Yes, Tony, I mean you. If you're denying it, you're lyin'.)

This is a genuine phenomenon: When people find a subject interesting, they learn better. Then we have kids who are struggling to function in school, who aren't learning nearly as much as their standardized tests say they should, who occasionally stumble on a topic that clicks for them and their attention span and alertness go way up.

The fact that it all magically comes together for our kids some of the time doesn't mean they are slacking off the rest of the day. It means they have found a respite, which is something you can use to their and your advantage. It doesn't mean the kid is otherwise lazy, willful, or stupid. It means you've got a ticket to getting this kid going, focused, and energetic at least some of the time.

But how do you explain this to the skeptic? Thing is, there's nothing wrong with being skeptical, and the skepticism doesn't automatically make the skeptic an enemy to you or your child. Nor does skepticism make them "bad" or "mean." It may, however, make them a royal pain in the neck.

Here's the key: ALL human beings can do difficult stuff some of the time and not at other times. When you've got a child with SPD, you've gotta look hard to find the underlying patterns which make this happen.

Admittedly, the idea that "he could do it if he tried" is partly true. People can do a lot if they pull all of their energy together for a specific goal. Motivation is actually important, as is the desire to do well.

But just because being motivated in a particular area and wanting to do well in general are good things, this doesn't make them sufficient for any given activity. There are so, so many times they aren't anything like enough.

Every year when I was a kid, we had the President's Physical Fitness test. Every kid who passed it got a certificate of some sort.

I wanted one of those certificates sooooooooooooo much. Not because I wanted the piece of paper, but because I wanted to be capable. I wanted to be able to run fast and jump high. I wanted to be a stellar kid. I wanted to be able to do more than two sit-ups!

Every dang year, I was determined, totally determined, to do better than I had before. When we girls had to do the bent-arm hang, one by one, I lined up with the others, taking deep breaths and going over the equivalent of "I think I can, I think I can, I think I can," in my mind ad infinitum.

I was motivated. I was determined. I was absolutely willing to take the pain of doing something really difficult, even if it made my arms ache for days, even if it took all my willpower to keep hanging in there when my muscles objected to the forced effort, even if I sweated and/or cried in front of the whole class and looked like a total lame-o.

And every year, I would get set up in the bent-arm position with determination burning in my soul. The teacher would get me set, warn me when she was about to let go so I'd be prepared, and then shes let go and start her stopwatch.

Except she never actually got to start the stopwatch. Every single year, I maintained the bent-arm hang for exactly zero seconds.

Not half a second. Not a tenth of a second. Zero seconds. Every year.

I cannot tell you how frustrating and humiliating this was. I've already given you an idea of what it's like to be picked last for EVERYTHING. Even if you haven't been there, you can, I suspect, imagine it pretty easily.

All of the determination and desire in the world meant nothing. I didn't have the upper-body strength, so I just couldn't support my own weight.

Incidentally (or not so incidentally), this was a shock that deeply upset me every year. I was, after all, determined! I had been told I don't know how many times that if you believe in yourself, you can do anything. I knew, from endless songs, books, and motivational posters than if you believe it, you can achieve it.

What never occurred to me is that I had missed a step. I had missed a lot of steps, actually. And this is the flaw in the idea that "If he wanted to do it, if he would just try harder, he would be able to."

You can't do stuff just because you want to and are determined. I wasn't being stubborn or lazy when I failed my physical fitness test. I was physically weak and for some mysterious reason as an 8-year-old I didn't have the capacity to create and regularly practice a comprehensive physical fitness regimen that would be safe and effective.

In fact, it may be a good thing that I didn't work out daily, because I had little idea of how the standard exercises we did in gym class were actually done correctly. My gross-motor coordination wasn't exactly spiffy, either. If I had "tried harder" by working out every day (which is so easy that everyone does it, right?) I probably would have messed up my back or wrenched my spleen or something.

And during my miserable failures in gym class (and my miserable failures in the classroom), I was often trying my best. I was putting in all of the effort I possibly could and failing anyway. And I was clueless about how to change things.

When we see kids with SPD (or ADHD, or learning disabilities—you know the list by now) who are failing to pay attention, answer questions, do craft projects, and otherwise tanking, we are not seeing kids who start out by not caring or not trying. We are dealing with kids who are humiliated and frustrated by their failures.

In fact, these failures are pretty much self-punishing. The resulting feelings (and playground teasing) are a built-in punishment that goes on and on. A time-out is temporary. An inner feeling that you are truly stupid and inadequate can last a lifetime. It will almost certainly last as long as it takes for someone to intervene and explain what's going on.

By the way, notice that I said that these are not kids who START OUT by not caring at all or by not trying. When you try your hardest over and over and fail, that's a teensy little bit demoralizing. And when you do the best you are currently capable of doing, when you are sweating blood and white-knuckling it through the school day, and the results are repeated scoldings and punishments, you don't keep trying hard forever.

When you try your level best and wind up with poor results or no results, that's frustrating. When you try your level best and the people around you are angry with you for not trying, you can feel like you're going crazy. You also feel like you are the most stupid and incompetent person in the world: If parents, teachers, and authority figures in general are sure that something would be easy if you "just tried," and you're trying so hard you feels like you are going to bust about a zillion capillaries in your brain, then the logical conclusion is that you are stupid. Stupid, stupid, stupid.

A lot of our kids wind up feeling dumb. The sound of a parent or teacher saying, "She could do it if she just tried" is the sound of a second-grader's heart breaking.

Did I think I was stupid? A lot of the time, yes. I would be wildly good at one thing and terrible at another, and I spent years of elementary school doing the same for academics as I did in gym: trying my hardest, working up all the belief in myself I possibly could, trying my hardest again, and never knowing whether success or failure would result.

Over the years it became glaringly obvious that my success or failure was not greatly influenced a heck of a lot by how hard I tried, at least partly because I genuinely didn't know what "trying harder" meant. Seriously, think about it. What do we mean when we ask kids to try harder? Does anyone outline a first simple step or two of what trying would involve or look like? Trying to use willpower and determination alone isn't actually very useful, but what other approach are these kids supposed to figure out?

I know a fellow who grew up with SPD, a fellow who is certainly more capable and intelligent than I am, who truly believed that he was intellectually disabled by the time he hit third grade. And when I say intellectually disabled, I'm using recent language. The only term available to him at the time for his self-labeling was "retarded."

He thought his parents were just too nice to tell him so.

Me, I veered wildly up and down, one minute convinced I was brilliant, and the next, that I was completely stupid and incompetent. I wound up being constantly afraid that something would happen publicly to prove, once and for all, that I was a big dummy.

So eventually not trying was not only the result of discouragement and constant misinformation ("You could do it if you just tried" is misinformation), but also the result of a desperate need to feel like it was possible that I was intelligent. In my childhood mindset, if you work for weeks on a project and it gets a "B," then it shows you aren't capable of getting an "A," and are therefore not too bright. If you throw something together at the last minute, then even a "D" doesn't mean you're stupid, it just meant you procrastinated too much.

When I say that "not trying" eventually became a mentality, a self-defense mechanism for me, don't think that meant just lying around not doing stuff and tossing off some work casually at the last minute. For kids who get shoved into this particular emotional place, what looks like just plain laziness and inertia from the outside is actually involves severe anxiety, and, often, depression.

"Not trying" actually meant having frequent panic/anxiety attacks in school, a constant feeling of being an innate failure, and intense, mental blowback when I did try to try.

Some years that meant bringing almost all of my books home from school every day for months, determined to finally start doing a proper job of studying. Those books were heavy and terrifying, but I lugged them home in the hopes that tonight would be different. I often spent my whole school day trying to work up the energy and determination to hit those books and be smart. But then I'd set the books on my desk at home and try to actually open one, and my whole brain would scream in fear and panic.

It wasn't a calculated thing. I may have just barely been aware that turning things in at the last minute was a bulwark against feeling dumb, but essentially I'd just fallen into a bad coping mechanism and couldn't find a way out.

"Not trying" was not about a lackadaisical approach to life or learning. My inner definition of laziness came out of teachers and others telling me I wasn't trying. Inside me, the idea of laziness was attached very strongly to that feeling of constant anxiety and killer depression. So I believed thoroughly that I was lazy, but my definition was not at all what people thought they were looking at.

Is There a Way Out?

There are things parents, teachers, and other folks who are dealing with children with SPD can do to help those children recover from feelings of incompetence or wildly inconsistent self-esteem. Among the most vital are listening to our kids, teaching them the skills they need to navigate a world that is not always SPD-friendly, and helping them understand what SPD is and what it means to them.

Listening to our kids is vital because they are the only folks on earth who know what they are actually experiencing. No, you can't be a great listener all of the time; sometimes what a child is saying is "Mommy, Mommy, Mommy, Mommy, hey, hey, hey, hey, can I have this?" Heck, kids do need to learn that there are limits to how often they can start a conversation with, "I beat the new Sonic game last night and here is every detail of everything I know about

Sonic and every bit of the new game and how it compares to these ten other games that I need to tell you all about right now."

Then again, do be aware of his interests. A child who can't say, "I feel lousy about having tantrums but don't have the skills to head them off," may be able to talk about how hard it is for Bruce Banner to control the Hulk, and how he feels like that sometimes.

But your children do need you to listen, especially when you're asking them questions. If the question is, "Why did you do that?" and the response is, "I don't know," instead of scolding him, believe him. When you ask your child a question, or if he is miraculously giving you data about himself and his problems spontaneously, listen. If he says, "I feel stupid," and you say, "Of course you're not stupid," then he knows you aren't listening. If he says, "I feel stupid," and you say, "Everyone feels stupid sometimes. Do you want to talk about it?" he might actually give you that vital information you need to help him.

Don't forget the old saw, "All behavior is communication." A child who is totally limp every time you try to put clothes on him is telling you his muscles aren't engaged, and he may not have good contact going with the world outside of his own head at the moment. When a child can't verbalize or isn't consciously aware of what's really going on, check out his behavior.

And no, you don't have to believe everything every child says—kids lie almost as much as adults do. And they don't always understand everything about what is going on inside them and in the world. I mean, I know a kid who swears that earthquakes are caused by gigantic underground farts, and I'm pretty sure that's not right.

I Know This Much Is True

I hope I've communicated that when you've got a kid with SPD (or ADD, or learning disability, or autism, or Asperger's), what you see is not necessarily what you get. When you see your child acting with what looks an awful lot like willful disobedience, stubbornness, and simple spite, you may be missing what is actually going on.

Sure, all kids do things you don't want them to do some of the time. There are no perfect people who are born always wanting to do what they are supposed to do who never ever fail to follow instructions and always perform all the tasks they should. Sometimes kids refuse to do things they can do. But not all of the time. In the case of kids with SPD, a lot of the time there's more to behavior than immediately meets the eye.

It is normal and human to assume that outward behavior is a sign of the inner person. We think that when a child is asked to do something difficult or unpleasant and says, "It's too hard," he might just be trying to get out of it. When a child says, "I can't do it," when it appears that he actually physically can, we usually assume he is avoiding the task at hand because he is lazy.

When you've got a kid with SPD and/or any of its accompanying disabilities, you can only learn what that child can do by paying attention to what he says and does.

I can't stress this enough. When a child with SPD says, "I can't," listen to him. This is especially true of a child you feel frustrated with. You and you alone have the power to change your own feelings from angry and frustrated to sympathetic and helpful, and the best way to do that is by listening. When a child can't cope with a situation, it's the adults who are there with him that have the power to make something happen differently. Do I have yet another scintillating example from my childhood? Of course I do!

When I was a child, every time I went to the dentist, it hurt like crazy to have my teeth cleaned and examined with those nasty little sharp instruments that they use to poke your teeth really hard. Every single time, I would tell the dentist that it hurt, and he would say, "You can't possibly feel that. It's just the noise that bothers you. If you just relax and stop worrying, it won't bother you at all."

Mind you, this was a dentist who was very competent, intelligent, and well trained. But he would tell me that I wasn't feeling pain I very much was, in fact, actually feeling.

Every single time.

What I learned was that when I was in real pain, there was no sympathy unless my pain fit preordained parameters. I learned that no matter how many times I pled with my dentist to be gentler, he didn't change what he was doing. My real sensations and experiences just plain didn't matter.

It was also really hard for me to brush my teeth or to floss. It was super-uncomfortable at minimum and often even painful. It was nasty and unpleasant and there were no positive sensations involved.

Since I had no control over the amount of pain I experienced at the dentist, I did what I could to control the thing I had a bit of a say in: I resisted regular brushing and flossing with all my might. I got cavities, but cavities involved getting lots of painkillers shot into my gums, so I didn't really mind getting a filling nearly as much as I minded the torture that was brushing my teeth.

Oh, the same dentist that insisted that I couldn't possibly feel the pain I really felt also scolded and lectured me about how I had to start brushing and flossing more often. So while I was being ignored and my very real pain brushed off (ha!), I was also being told I was a very bad kid.

From my point of view, there was nothing good about dental hygiene or preventative dental care. There was no one to say, "Oh, I know brushing your teeth is hard, but if you do it as often as you can stand to, that's good enough for starters."

In fact, no one ever, ever, ever suggested that if I missed a day or two it wasn't a horrible disaster, and I that should just keep doing my best to brush my teeth as often as I could manage. It was always, "You have to do this excruciating thing on a strict schedule and that's how it is."

They didn't actually tell me that the Baby Jesus cried every time I failed to floss, but they came close.

I didn't start brushing my teeth daily until the horrific morning breath that adolescence brought made it unbearable not to. By that time, I could brush in the shower, and the hot water helped me stay calm and distracted me with a pleasant sensation to muffle the nastiness of brushing. Even then, I would not floss because that was just too much pain to handle.

(Since I live in Southern California, I'd like to assure my fellow SoCalers that I no longer brush my teeth in the shower. Be water wise, everybody!)

If my dentist had listened to me and understood that I was in pain, things could have been seriously different. I know this because as I got older dentists started admitting that sensitive teeth do exist and that when a person says, "Ow, that hurts!" the thing to do is listen to them.

At this point, I make my own dental appointments and am quite well behaved during them. I know it is safe for me to tolerate minor pain during the cleaning, because if I need a break or if I need to stop altogether, the hygienist or dentist will actually stop. I can handle a little bit of pain now that I know I have more control of the situation.

It is way easier to do something difficult if the people around you are supportive and you know that they will listen to you.

So, as a kid, I could have said, point-blank, "It's too hard to floss my teeth," and no one would have believed me. That meant no credit at all for doing something painful and difficult. Avoiding the pain was the most logical and functional choice I was capable of making at the time.

Can you listen? Can you give your child that much credit? If he says, "That hurts," will you say, "Okay, let's try something else," or will you say, "Don't be silly, that can't hurt!" Will he get gaslighted every single day by every adult he interacts with, or will someone listen and observe enough to hear what he is actually trying to communicate?

Listening, observing, and learning will take you a lot farther than scolding will. Not only that, you can avoid doing a lot of harm when you take the least-damaging course of action.

The Least Possible Damage

It's important for parents and teachers to think about whether and when there could be real damage in ignoring or disbelieving straightforward statements from children. Here's an example with a child who has a different disability: A friend of mine has a daughter who has had type 1 diabetes since she was 2 years old. Let that sink a minute.

This is a young girl who has never known a day when she did not have to pay attention to her blood sugar and food intake, nor a day when she could chose food on a whim. She has always been this way, diabetes is part of her life, and she understands that she needs to be alert to possible issues with her blood sugar in order to stay healthy.

One day during gym class, she went to the teacher and told him she needed a snack because her blood sugar was low. She explained that she was diabetic.

The gym teacher thought she was lying, so he refused to let her leave class to get a snack. She wanted him to ask the school nurse, but he didn't.

Said gym teacher got his you-know-what handed to him by a very angry mother the next day. It was epic.

But the point of this story is not that one teacher was being thick. It's the fact that he picked the most dangerous and hostile course of action over the simplest and most repairable.

If he had let her get a snack because it was possible that she was being truthful (as she was), then he would have been doing the minimum amount necessary to treat her decently.

On the other hand, if he had let her get a snack and then checked and found out she was not diabetic, she would be in trouble. She might lose a few recesses or have to stay after school as a punishment for lying.

Either way, the consequences of letting her get a snack would not be dire or cause serious problems. On the other hand, the consequences of not letting her get a snack could be serious—as in serious medical complications can result from not doing so.

Similar situations arise with children who have SPD. If the child avoids a task because it is painful or because he doesn't understand how to do it, the best thing to do is start by listening to him. It's the least damaging, most helpful way possible to find out what is actually going on. You don't have to commit to believing him forever just to listen for a bit.

Mind you, if he says, "I can't possibly do this without a hundred chocolate bars and a dozen bearers to carry me on an elaborate sedan chair," then maybe he's fibbing. But you'd know that, wouldn't you?

Serious complications can result from not listening to a child. If a child learns, over and over again, that he lives in a world where no one trusts him and all of his pleas for help and support are ignored, it can leave him in an emotional place you wouldn't wish on your worst enemy.

Some kids do become liars just because no one believes them anyway. Others become confused and hurt, withdrawing from humans as much as they can. Others are so frustrated that they "blow up" with rage, simply because they can't cope with the combination of physical, mental, and emotional pain.

It hurts. Let me be more specific about that: It hurt me. It hurt that when I tried to tell my parents and teachers why I was stymied, they assumed I was lying. It hurt that after I had been told to ask a trusted adult for help with almost any problem, none of those adults listened. It hurt when I had severe anxiety attacks that stopped me cold and the people around me identified that as "laziness."

I became lazy, in a way. I avoided any task that seemed difficult because there was no support, no help, when I just "tried my best." Instead, I got told that my very best meant that I was "just goofing off" or "not taking her work seriously."

There were a lot of things I did not know how to do, and I was terrified to attempt to do anything without clear directions. Even when I had been given directions, I didn't always understand them correctly, and when I hit the wall, it was "Jennifer does not try" and "Jennifer does not work up to expectations." Trust me, being called an "underachiever" hurts, especially when you are all but sweating blood to make it through the school day.

As previously indicated, I'm not telling you this to get sympathy for me. When I look back at the people who did and said those things, and I know for sure they simply had no idea what was going on. All of those teachers would have gladly helped me if they had understood what I needed. None of them would have deliberately obstructed me.

(Okay, I did have one teacher in grade school who was so inflexible she wouldn't have been able to change, but she was just a limited person. If I couldn't forgive that, I would have a teeny-tiny, dried-up soul by now.)

My parents, while they often didn't get it, did a lot of things that helped me. They brought tons of interesting books into the house; they watched interesting and exciting television and encouraged me to watch it, too; they encouraged outdoor play and built the biggest, coolest sandbox a kid ever had. More importantly, in those situations in which they did understand the kind of problems I was having, they worked to help me and to help me learn to help myself.

It still hurt when I tried to tell people about the real problems I was having and they would not listen. I don't need anyone to feel sorry for me or for the child I was, but I do really hope that adults can develop understanding and sympathy for the children going through those same problems now.

So, for those kids, let me give you just one more example from my own life. Somewhere, right now, there is a kid going through these same emotions.

When I was a kid, Mr Snuffleupagus was my favorite *Sesame Street* character, which is saying a lot. I loooooved Mr Snuffleupagus, and I enjoyed every minute I watched him.

But I never watched him all the way to the end. During each segment he was in, I was poised, tense, ready to run. Because back then, at the end of each sequence, the "gag" was that Mr Snuffleupagus would walk away just before some of the adults came over, and none of the adults would believe Big Bird when he said Mr Snuffleupagus had been there. They all thought Mr S was imaginary, and they let Big Bird know that's what they thought.

Over time, Mr Snuffleupagus was responsible for stuff that the adults weren't happy about, and they always blamed Big Bird and thought he was fibbing when he said it wasn't him.

I refused to watch a Mr Snuffleupagus segment to the end. As soon as it looked like he might walk away, I darted out of the room as fast as I could, and I stayed out until I was absolutely sure it was over. I preferred missing 10 minutes of Sesame Street to the possibility that I might have to see the adults on the show as they refused to believe Big Bird.

I graduated from high school in 1984, so I was pretty much (sort of) an adult, 19 years old, in November of 1985. It was then that I read in TV Guide that the folks who make *Sesame Street* had decided it was about time the adults found out that Mr Snuffleupagus was real and Big Bird had not been lying. The reason given was that they were worried children who were victims of abuse might think they wouldn't be believed if they went to adults for help.

I was actually emotionally overcome when I read this. Even after all of those intervening years. There was joy and anger and relief all bundled up together just about bursting out of my heart and brain. I was genuinely ferklempt.

And that's how much it means for these kids to be heard. That's how much kids with SPD need to be believed, need to be listened to, and need to know that there are people they can go to when they have real problems, real pains, and real fears.

Our kids deserve to be listened to.

Knowledge Is Power!

Another thing that helps children in a zillion ways is having some under-standing of sensory processing themselves. Just as *Schoolhouse Rock* taught us, knowledge is power!

Knowledge can come in several forms. The speech therapists who did so much for me during my school career gave me a huge amount of knowledge about a group of sounds that utterly confused me. Breaking down sounds, sights, and movements so that a child knows more about incoming sensory input can help him become un-disabled. Jumbled hearing, chaotic move-ments, and other nasty issues that make life harder can respond super-well to a therapist (or parent) who is willing and able to break down exactly what those things consist of.

What other things can knowledge help with? Well, there's the basic issue of understanding that nondangerous situations can cause panic attacks and that the smartest thing to do during a panic attack is use basic self-soothing methods to calm down.

It is really important to help our kids learn to take deep breaths, because if you aren't in touch with your own body, it can take quite a bit of practice and effort to do so. I had plenty of teachers and other adults who would tell me to "take a deep breath" when I was upset, but I would take shallow breaths into my upper chest because I had no idea how to do better than that.

When I was a teen I ran across a book about yoga, of all things, and it had an explanation and diagrams showing how you take a deep breath by expanding your diaphragm as you breathe. It was a revelation!

There is a reason it helps to take deep breaths when you panic. It helps slow your elevated heart rate, which helps slow down the adrenaline pumping through your veins, which helps with the physical aspects of panic.

As a kid, I genuinely didn't believe that taking deep breaths would help me when I panicked, because no one had explained that to me. I missed out on a great way to calm down, which is a bit of a bummer, but the young SPuDster in your life could use the information right now.

As a child, I always "knew" that my panic and anger meant something IMPORTANT was wrong and I absolutely had to lash out to protect myself. This was not helpful. It meant I was often powerless to help myself handle difficult situations.

Knowledge is power.

The Parallax View

Another advantage of giving a child information about SPD and his own functioning is that it can help him see the world in a different way.

When I was growing up, my anger always felt not only real but overwhelmingly important. Erratic movements in my field of vision, cacophonic background noises, or the feeling of the breeze on my arms when I changed over from long sleeves to short in the spring could make me feel very much like something was wrong, and when someone or something pushed me over the edge, it felt like it was VITAL for me to deal with it.

Once I got pushed over that edge, I wasn't simply coping with the feeling of fight/flight/freeze. It felt like the person who had hurt or bothered me had done so on purpose and they had to pay. Only my righteous anger could mend the wrongs of the world, by ensuring that person would never, ever do it again.

I was genuinely afraid that if I somehow had been able to contain my anger, people would hurt me more and more. If there were no consequences, then what would slow them down? I had no idea of how I could possibly control my temper, but I was also afraid of what might happen if I did. Then again, that might just have been my ego's way of justifying angry outbursts that came out of nowhere and seemed beyond my control.

It is hard, super duper hard, for anyone to stay calm once her body is freaking out. It is not at all easy to learn not to clobber the person who has pushed you too far, especially if it is a classmate who has learned how to push those buttons and cannot resist the temptation to do so. (Yes, sometimes kids are mean to other kids on purpose.)

It helped me very much when I learned that SPD can create a situation where my anger and pain are not necessarily signs that I need to mend the situation and put the world back on its axis through my own righteous fury.

No, a child is not immediately going to develop self-control in all situations by knowing this. But if he knows that part of the problem is sensory in nature and gets coaching on how to calm himself down, he has a better chance of learning to cope better and of (eventually) developing more self-control.

The kid who knows that sensory overload isn't a sign that he has to "fix" the world has a lot more power. That kid can seek a way to get out of the situation temporarily, can practice deep breathing and mindfulness techniques to cope better when he can't leave the situation, and can even have the confidence of knowing that while others may not understand right now, there is nothing wrong with him, even if he's being thrown off by the situation.

This is not instantaneous. In particular, it doesn't work at all if the adults around him start saying things like, "It's just your SPD, it's not anything important," while he is in the midst of a meltdown. A meltdown is seldom a teachable moment.

A lot of parents worry about kids getting diagnosed with SPD (or attention-deficit disorder, or learning disability, or autism spectrum disorder) because they naturally worry about labels. Is a diagnosis just going to drag their kid down? Then they worry about the kid finding out about the label he's got, because they naturally don't want him to think something is wrong with him.

But without official labels, kids get labeled anyway. And without knowing their own official label, kids label themselves.

My internal labels included *dumb*, *thick*, *angry*, and *clumsy* (all significantly less popular dwarves). I often swerved wildly between thinking I was smart (like right after an Algebra I test) and thinking I was stupid (right after trying to hit a tennis ball or read a novel aimed above an 11-year-old level). My self-esteem spent an unholy amount of time in the toilet.

Today, I look at self-esteem and self-confidence as just two more areas that have been helped a ton by knowing I have SPD. Weirdly, having more self-esteem has made me (slightly) less egotistical and selfish. I guess if you don't feel like you're under attack, you stop being quite so defensive.

I know that when I'm in a really crowded place, I'm going to be less able to make decisions or communicate. It's not because I'm dumb, it's because I can only do so much processing at a time and those situations can overload my brain a bit, which means any bout of stupidity that I experience is purely temporary.

It is a zillion times better to have your internal label be something like, "Oh, I have SPD, and it screws me up sometimes, but I can work with that," than to think you are just clumsy and stupid. It's also easier to overcome problems when you know what they are.

Does this mean you should sit your child down for a thorough explanation of what SPD is and how it affects him? Depends on the kid. What a child needs to know varies not only from kid to kid but also from day to day and task to task.

Figuring out what your child needs to understand and is able to comprehend is a daunting task, but you're better off trying to communicate than hoping to keep the whole thing a big secret. There is nothing that torpedoes a child's trust in the world more than finding out that adults have been systematically lying to him.

In fact, knowledge is power in a zillion different ways, and you can help a child improve his sensory processing if you can find ways to communicate about what is going on and how the brain develops new connections and better functioning.

Too Much Self-Esteem?

It is possible for a child to overestimate himself too much, which can happen as another side effect of a child who is ignorant of his own sensory differences and who has been gas-lighted once too often.

I was lucky: As a child, I believed there were things in the outside world that triggered my anger, but I also thought there was some kind of internal problem inside of me that made me wrong or messed up. That meant I didn't entirely blame my anger on others.

I thought my anger came from inside as well as out, and felt the underlying problems were so deep and complex that I couldn't get to them. I was smart enough to (usually) reject the just-so stories common in psychiatry—you know, your mom toilet-trained you too young so you have anger issues, that kind of nonsense—but I did read a few too many pop psychology books and believed there was some kind of imbalance or neurosis inside me messing things up.

Why do I feel lucky that I thought something was wrong with me? Because there is a much worse alternative.

See, there are kids who are smart but lack self-awareness. It is super hard to develop good self-awareness when you can barely tell where your own body is, never mind sitting through a day at school. And some of those kids have it worse than me.

I had low self-esteem and sometimes often little esteem for humans in general, but I didn't think it was only and always everyone else's fault when things went wrong. Some kids, at some point, decide it is everyone else's fault and that they are not ever at fault themselves. That's the long, slow, downhill road to Painsville.

In the Asperger's world, this is called "being in god mode." This is the kid who has decided that he is right and everyone else is wrong, and that's all there is to it. I'm using "he" here, but it happens with plenty of "shes," too.

A smart kid with sensory issues can often, to some little extent, determine that he is seeing things differently than other people. Sensory issues can make the unexpected upsetting, so a lot of kids with SPD develop control-freak tendencies.

When you get a control freak who hears other people telling him the situation is not what he thinks it is, sometimes the way the poor kid knows copes is by deciding that he is right and everybody else is wrong. It's a crude defense mechanism that can get out of hand.

But whether a child blames himself for his problems, blames others, or blames different people at different times, the antidote to the blame game is the same: Educate the child. While a good sensory diet and appropriate occupational therapy are great, educating the child can have a big, big effect.

When I saw that my anger was coming from intense sensory overload, I realized that this meant my anger didn't make me a bad person, any more than it meant other people were being bad. Feeling like I needed to develop better coping skills and figure out how to respond better was a tremendous improvement over my previous assumptions. Instead of either being broken or surrounded by crazy people, I was simply someone who needed to learn to handle things better.

And I knew I could learn new skills, because I had done it before. In fact, my parents had taught me life skills that helped me immeasurably while growing up with SPD.

Crude but Effective

Children, teens, and adult SPuDsters will all develop their own coping methods to deal with sensory issues, especially because each of them is coping with the unique nature of their own SPD and running into the barriers that their personal, specific expression of SPD creates.

SPD can often cause very real problems that are difficult to express or describe. You yourself have no doubt experienced how variable sensory processing is, even when it is well within the normal range.

It is, for example, very common for humans to have variable levels of sensitivity throughout their daily lives. The noisy fan that you ignored when you came to the office well rested in the morning might drive you crazy after a particularly tense meeting with the boss. The task that seemed nearly impossible at 11 AM looks much more straightforward after a good lunch.

If you're going on no sleep, you'll be crankier and probably have noticeably different sensory responses than when you've had a good night's rest. Those different body states and emotional states have a huge effect on how well you take in and respond to sensory input, whether you have SPD or not.

We all know the classic example, where you're driving in an unfamiliar area and you suddenly realize you need to retrace your route to find the right turn-off—and as you look for that street sign or ramp, you find yourself turning the radio down. Somehow you need quiet so you can see where you are. Because humans.

With SPD, it isn't just the usual effects of stress and tiredness that play havoc with sensory processing, it's also which bits of sensory processing are actually there in a given situation.

As a kid, I was known for the fact that I was a horrible person to deal with first thing in the morning. When I was first awakened, I was nasty as heck, and chewing out and otherwise verbally abusing anyone who had the temerity to attempt to, say, tell me I needed to get ready for school.

In fact, my waking-up skills were so incredibly bad that my mom resorted to getting me an alarm clock when I was in the second grade. My mom is a brilliant woman who got me to do all kinds of things I didn't want to do or thought I couldn't do. She could not get me to act like a human being when I woke up. First thing in the morning, I was in ravening angry yeti mode, and there was no way to deal with it other than to stay away from me.

I woke up with only a few parts of my brain coherent—the yelling lobe and the fury quadrant were wide awake first, but nothing having to do with logic or self-preservation was up and running yet. (The basic instinct for self-preservation would have prevented me from yelling at my mom so much when the outcome was going to be so very not good for me.)

The process of waking up was always hard to do (there's a song in there somewhere), and when I first woke up, I was in a largely under-responsive sensory state. And I needed to change that. If I wanted to get moving, I had to do something to get that sensory input processing going!

So as I got older and needed to get myself to school (no one else got up early enough for me to rely on them to get me to the early bus for choir practice), I started resorting to strong input. Seriously strong input, suitable for someone in a somnambulant state who nonetheless craved something, anything, to get out of that all-encasing mental shell.

When I was a teen, it was simple: I took the world's hottest showers. I would start the shower with the water as hot as I could comfortably tolerate it, and then crank it up hotter, bit by bit, until I was able to tolerate A REAL- LY HOT SHOWER. I was generally bright pink by the time I got out.

Of course, when I showered, I closed the door to the bathroom. This meant Step 2 of waking up was right there waiting to be implemented: Open up that bathroom door all the way in one swoosh, so I'd be hit by a blast of cold air that would have startled a woolly yak.

So I would start out with little connection to the world around me, barely on speaking terms with my body, usually hitting the snooze button five or six times without any knowledge of doing so. I was not dealing with input in any meaningful way until I blasted myself to life with the hot-and-cold treat- ment, which I loved.

And then I'd be awake. Super-awake, a lot of the time, and usually some- what panic stricken about the fact that I had to get to the bus stop NOWN- OWNOW! I'd hear every creak of every step on the way down to the kitchen. If I missed the early bus, that meant taking the regular bus, and that was a living hell because …

Because I'd switched modes. I'd awakened with little awareness of the world around me, limp and listless, dragging my less-than-enthused body to the shower, but once I woke myself up with the really hot water, I was no longer numb to the world: I was painfully aware of it, and my sluggish, un- der-responsive start had given way to serious over-responsivity.

Once I was awake, a bus full of laughing, talking, moving, and generally not at all quiet kids was a nightmare. The early bus had far fewer kids, and they were generally not awake enough to be rowdy.

If I took that early bus, once I got to school I was in a very sparse- ly populated building where I interacted with just about no one who wasn't a music nerd. The halls were empty, I went to my locker alone and in peace, and I got myself to the choir room with very little interaction or interference.

Once I woke up, I was really awake, which means every little thing was a distraction. Choir was ideal, because it's an activity that a bunch of people do in parallel—there is little as everybody is actually performing independently, just next to each other.

(I don't think I could have handled the veritable social butterflies of the marching band and band front. Those guys were crazy.)

So by 7:30 AM, I had gone through states of under-responsivity, sensory craving (desperately grasping at strong input, but still out of order), and over-responsivity. The triple threat.

A lot of kids combine under-responsivity and over-responsivity in the same moments. The kid who barely notices when the rest of the class takes out their books can also be the kid who jumps and freaks out when someone taps him on the shoulder. The kid who seems almost limp in gym class can be the kid who is so sensitive to the sounds and smells of the cafeteria that he still feels nauseated an hour after lunch.

There is, I'm pretty sure, no combination that can't exist, and two kids with the same diagnosis sitting next to each other can be experiencing the world in very different ways. They may also be using very different coping mechanisms to go with their different needs.

Take me and my sister. We were two kids growing up with SPD with the same parents, in the same house and in the same school district, and we had totally different sensory wants and needs.

One great thing my parents did was allow us to decorate our own rooms. They even told us we could pick out any color of paint for the walls and any color of carpet.

I got home from school every day drained and nervous, and in fact much of the time I was on edge. I picked a soothing cool green for my bedroom walls, with a similarly green carpet: serene, mellow, calming. Very Zen.

My sister, on the other hand, picked the brightest orange imaginable for her walls. I mean BRIGHT! I'm pretty sure it was bright enough to burn out your eyeballs if you spent enough time in there—heck, bright enough to keep me away from her room the vast majority of the time (not a bad side effect from her point of view).

Seriously, it was ORANGE. I felt like the walls were vibrating with color when I looked in there, even with the lights off.

My sister also picked out the perfect carpet color: vibrant purple. That would have been ideal for her, but my parents vetoed it.

Yes, my parents are awesome, but they shouldn't have reneged on their promise to let us pick any colors we wanted. My sister Cath wanted a bright orange room with purple carpet, and she should have had it. Even if it did hurt the resale value.

The thing is, once I got my sensory jolt in the morning, I was way more likely to be over-responsive than under-responsive, so a nice soothing color made my room hospitable for me. My sister, on the other hand, needed something a bit more intense. Her particular pattern of combined under- and over-responsivity called for a different kind of input.

Seriously, they should have popped for the purple carpet.

So, two kids, same family, same house, both with SPD, and we sought out completely different kinds of input a lot of the time. And we both combined over- and under-responsivity, but in very different ways.

Incidentally, we both wrongly "diagnosed" as kids. I was considered an underachiever with a terrible temper that went off with absolutely no provocation; Catherine was, in what has to be the world's most ironic label, considered a bit slow and lacking in the smarts department. This is like calling a soaring eagle a mollusk.

If your child has developed coping methods and seeks helpful sensory input in ways that (*a*) work and (*b*) do not actually damage either the child or other people, support and encourage that. You might learn a lot about your child's sensory profile by observing and tolerating these things.

Chapter 12

What Helped & Hurt at School

One thing about growing up with SPD is that the OK through 12 world is not necessarily a friendly place for those who don't have standard input systems. There are a tremendous number of assumptions that teachers and administrators make about how children experience the school day and what those children's subsequent behaviors mean. Most of the more typical kids pick up fairly well on those expectations, and so their reactions are based on pretty much the same assumptions.

Here's the shorter version: The student with SPD is often a very square peg in a surprisingly well-standardized round hole.

Looking at my own experience growing up, one of the most important facts about my interactions with teachers is that the vast majority of my teachers wanted to help me learn and would have been willing to bend a little—if only someone had known what to ask of them.

This is usually (not always, but usually) true today, as well. Most teachers do want to actually teach their students, and they might even like to know if there are small changes they can make that would make a big difference to their students with SPD.

In particular, teachers are often willing to make changes or offer options that will help kids with SPD learn if parents and therapists can encourage them without overwhelming them.

That's tough to do. It is very difficult for a parent who has spent weeks, months, or years learning how to help his or her child to be calm, polite, and self-assured when faced with a teacher who has no idea of what to do with this particular child. Especially if that teacher has seen so many difficult 9-year-olds and so many difficult parents that she is skeptical of information coming from relative amateurs.

It might be helpful if parents have some ideas about what really does help and what seriously hurts when a child with SPD is trying to learn and/or survive with his sanity intact in a school setting.

Yes, this is another excuse for me to tell you thrilling tales from my own childhood—but again, there is a point. Several points, in fact.

Often a teacher who did great things for me also did sucky things that I found excruciatingly painful. These teachers weren't "against" me, but they had habits or assumptions that were not so helpful. And even great teachers can do seemingly dumb things.

My second grade teacher was one of the most wonderful, warm, and intelligent people I have ever had the pleasure to meet. And she very nearly drove me out of my mind.

She had one thing in her classroom that was ideal for a sensory over-responsive child: a "learning station" that was simply a small reading area in a corner, separated from the rest of the room by dividers. In fact, there was a whole cluster of learning stations, but most of them involved some social interaction and were open to the main part of the noisy, chaotic classroom.

Think about what it is like to be a sensory over-responder in the typical second-grade classroom. There are colorful posters on the walls, carefully designed educational bulletin board displays that change with the seasons, and desks grouped so as to encourage children to work together. It's a living hell. My personal hell.

And then there was the reading station. It was small and cozy, and because we got to pick which station we wanted to go to each day, any child who wanted to be boisterous or play with others would pick another station. The reading station was just a few kids reading while sitting as far from each other as space allowed and ignoring each other completely. In other words, heaven.

The rule was simple: Once we finished our worksheets in the morning, we could pick any station to spend our "free time" in. Once a station was full, you had to pick another; it was all on a first-come, first-served basis.

I raced through those worksheets to be absolutely sure of getting to the reading corner first. I would have rather slit my wrists than go to any of the other stations. The other stations involved interacting with other children and being in the chaos of the larger classroom.

So, every day, I picked the reading station. And as the school year wore on, my second-grade teacher would pull aside during the day and ask if maybe I could try the other stations sometimes.

It seemed like a reasonable request, and I said that I'd try. But I didn't. I couldn't.

After the chaos of lining up on the playground and the torture of sitting in small groups so that I had to consciously work to hear the teacher while being distracted by the other children's movements, after sitting in a classroom full of visual aids and bright, cheery colors, I could not face any other station. I needed to retreat, to be someplace quieter and less chaotic, and the reading station offered me the one and only chance I would have all day to do that.

The problem with this was that the stations were designed for learning, and the assumption underlying the setup was that any given child would choose different stations on different days and more or less wind up spending at least a little time in each of them. Those stations were actually part of the curriculum, an important part of learning and reinforcing the material we were expected to cover.

I didn't know that, and of course my teacher never told me. She just kept taking me aside and trying to talk me into going to different stations. And I kept going to the one station that wasn't painful for me, so I kept missing out on practicing important skills I needed to effectively master the second grade and prepare to tackle the third.

This seems to be a normal setup. Teachers unknowingly tie vital parts of the curriculum to tasks which are not suited to kids who have SPD. In particular, teachers assume that children learn better in environments with lots of bright colors and visual aids and that children should also get the opportunity to do group work in a cooperative setting. This is, in my not-so-humble opinion, awful.

The reality is that most children will be a bit excited but not over-stimulated by the use of color and frequently changed bulletin boards. And apparently, typical children can survive doing group work even in second grade.

The same sort of classroom can be troublesome for the under-responsive child as well. When there are lots of bright posters and visual displays competing for their attention, they may get "woken up" a bit but not be able to pick out each item when they need to. The lack of contrast—the consistency of the overall educational setting—means there may not be enough oomph in any one input for the under-responsive child to focus on any particular thing.

Sensory-seeking children may love such a classroom, but without an organized way to approach the chaos, they may not be able to make sense of it.

All I'm saying is that the standard cheery, bright, stimulating classroom is not really always ideal for all children. It helps a lot when teachers in those classrooms understood that.

The help I needed to work well in my second grade classroom was simple: I needed to retreat from the chaos regularly, and I needed to have my learning process separated from the need to visit the stations that gave me no chance to retreat.

I had no idea of any of this. When I told my teacher I would try to try some of the other stations, I meant it. I wanted to please her. It's just that when I was faced with the actual situation, I couldn't do what she wanted. Not wouldn't, couldn't.

Here's the key: If a child needs a quiet place to learn, you can pretty much stick anything she needs in that quiet place, and have a reasonable chance of her looking at it.

If the book corner had included books on the subjects I was supposed to review, I would have read them. It would have been a thousand times easier to look at specific books that my teacher suggested to me than to leave my safe haven.

If there had been a quiet place to unwind or an errand to run, I would have been more together by the time we had to pick our stations, and instead of seeking a retreat, I might have been able to handle what was happening in the main classroom.

Most importantly, if my teacher had understood the general sorts of problems caused by SPD, she would have been willing to find ways to help me, and to help other kids who were different. This is probably the most important thing a child, teen, or adult with SPD can come to understand. It can make life and school that much less scary.

I loved this particular teacher. I knew she liked each and every child in her class, including me. She drove me nuts on a fairly regular basis (and I'm sure I returned the favor), but she loved kids and I loved her.

It meant a lot to me that she usually assumed that I wanted to do things right and to be a good student. There is a huge difference between a teacher who lacks the information to help a child and a teacher who simply dismisses the "problem child" by blaming the child and/or the parents.

In third grade I had a new teacher, of course, and her classroom was a lot less chaotic. Our seats were kept in neat rows, so we never had to face other children while we worked. It should have been better, but it was much worse, because that teacher believed that all of my problematic behaviors were deliberate and purposeful.

My third-grade teacher consistently assumed that all of my failures to conform were willful. I honestly think she believed I could have done what she asked of me if I had just "tried harder."

SPD can cause a child a lot of pain and confusion. Pain and confusion get worse worse when your emotional state gets worse.

No matter what Patrick Swayze said in Roadhouse, pain does hurt. Pain also gets more intense when you're under stress, and even more intense when you are afraid.

When a child knows that her teacher will like her and believe what she is saying, that child will still suffer pain when there is too much nasty input. The too-loud colors will still be too loud, the video with the noisy music in the background will still make no sense, and the unpleasant feeling of confusion that comes with directions given too fast, with too many words and too many gestures, will still be there.

But, if the teacher genuinely likes children (and can fake it decently on the days when she feels lousy) and is willing to admit that maybe, just maybe, this kid isn't purposely acting out at random for no reason other than to drive her crazy, that child has a far less scary and painful situation than the same child with a teacher who has judged her and found her wanting.

And yes, I do happen to have a very specific example of that very situation.

While having a fifth-grade teacher who was honest and caring did not fix my SPD, it did make a huge difference in what I could attempt and how much I succeeded.

Unfortunately, he also regularly pulled one of the nastiest tricks you could ever play on a kid with SPD. He wanted us to hold our pens with a correct grip during handwriting lessons—"correct" meaning a relatively light grip, such as a person with really good fine-motor coordination would have.

To (ahem) encourage this, he would assign us some pages of handwriting practice and then wait until we were all more or less absorbed in our writing. He would then walk around the classroom very quietly, and every so often he would come up behind a completely oblivious student and TRY TO YANK THE PEN OUT OF HER HAND!!!!

The idea was that if you were holding your pen correctly, the pen would come right out of your grip. If you were holding your pen "badly" (tightly), your entire arm would go up, as well.

Yes, this man actually snuck up behind me and yanked my arm up into the air while I was writing. Over and over, week after week, month after month.

As mentioned previously, sensory over-responsivity often causes a heightened fight-or-flight reaction. Every time Mr. R tried to yank the pen from my hand, I would instantly go into fight-or-flight mode, terrified, full of adrenaline, heart pounding, breath quickened, pale as a ghost.

It was horrible. Every single time we had penmanship practice, I focused as intently as I was able to on not clutching my pen tightly—but I didn't have the fine-motor skills needed for success. I inevitably reverted to my usual death-grip on the pen—something like a cross between a baby grasping and pulling on long hair and the grip of a frail, elderly person holding onto a friend for support. Yes—that tight.

And my iron grip meant I got my arm yanked up, again and again. I'm not sure it would have been all that great if I had a looser grip, being as that would still mean having my pen suddenly yanked out of my hand from behind.

And yet, I loved my fifth-grade teacher. I would have crawled through broken glass for him—and I basically did the SPD equivalent on a regular basis. Even his truly horrible penmanship teaching strategy did not make me see him as an enemy.

You see, he really cared, and he admitted that he didn't know how to help me.

When our class went to work on our reports in the library, I was not able to get anything done. Being in a smallish library with 17 other kids working independently was just too overstimulating. There was no regularity to it, kids would get up and go to the shelves or the card catalog (Note: Get off my lawn), they would read or flip through books, they would write then read then stand up then settle in somewhere else—it was like gosh-darned Times Square in there.

So I bopped around the library, interrupting other kids and generally making a nuisance of myself. I had no idea I was a nuisance, because it was obviously (to me) a situation where no one could possibly be getting any work done. I mean, if I talked to the other kids, I was, from my point of view, rescuing them from the horrific boredom of the entire exercise in futility that was working in a crowded library.

Mr. R asked to speak with me out in the hall. First, he explained that I was bothering the other kids, who were trying to work and didn't want to be interrupted.

This was information I did not previously have. I genuinely had no idea that I was bothering people, and I was totally willing to stop doing that. I had no problem going to the other end of the library and reading on my own while they were working, and Mr. R said that would be appropriate and helpful.

Then he asked me a question. Saints alive, hallelujah and begorrah, he asked me THE most important question ever.

"I know you are smart enough to do the work in this class, and I know you are struggling and genuinely having trouble doing that. I really don't know why that is. Can you think of anything I could do that would help you do better?"

How do I even express how huge this was? This was not fake, this was not anything like the rote responses I had gotten from other teachers. This was not, "Why won't you try harder" or "You've just got to stop goofing off."

This was a teacher telling me he was in the same boat I was. He knew I was struggling, and he didn't know why—just like me. He asked me for suggestions. He admitted his ignorance and asked me for help.

I had no idea what to tell him. I knew I was having all kinds of trouble learning and genuinely didn't know why. But he didn't know why, either, and he wanted to be helpful. That was, for me, enough. Not enough for me to do much better (all of my problems were still there), but enough for me to feel human again.

I told him that I didn't understand, either, and that I didn't know what to ask for. He told me that if I thought of anything, he would appreciate it if I would let him know.

He didn't fix my life. He didn't even fix any one component of my school day. But, instead of punishing me for bugging the other kids, he gave me an alternative (Can you sit over there and read instead of interrupting others?) and instead of lecturing me about my bad attitude, he admitted his ignorance.

Instead of lecturing me about trying harder, he actually made it possible for me to try harder. He allowed me to feel like a confused kid instead of a just a screw-up.

I learned more in the classrooms of teachers who knew they didn't understand me than in the classrooms of teachers who thought they did. That matters.

Crime and Punishment

One issue that comes up between SPuDsters and their schools again and again is punishment versus rehabilitation. Teachers and principals naturally use punishments to modify student behavior, but they may not pick up on the fact that some patterns of punishment won't have the desired effect on a kid with SPD.

Mind you, I am big on rules and consequences. The fact that my mom enforced the house rules with things like revocation of privileges (meaning loss of access to vital commodities like cookies and TV) was actually very important, because not only did it work, it also meant I knew my mom had a will of iron and was not to be messed with. There is a really warm, secure feeling you get when you know your parents are strong enough to handle difficult situations.

You can influence a child very positively with well-thought-out rules and consequences. It's a behavioral approach, and the thing about behavioral approaches is that they can work really well when they are realistic. If a kid can, with a bit of effort, climb a ladder and hang from a jungle gym, you can, in fact, bribe him to do just that, and that's cool.

But you can't change a child's neurological functioning with a poorly thought out behavioral approach, and trying will frustrate everyone involved. I've had multiple parents say to me, "They send my son to the principal's office at least once a day because of his behavior." The natural question is, "Does that work?" And in those cases, the answer is always, "No, he does the exact same thing anyway."

In those cases, the behavioral approach is not working in either direction. The child isn't changing his behavior, and neither is the teacher. If you send a child to the office 50 times for the same behavior and nothing changes, then maybe sending him to the office isn't working—pure behaviorism would indicate here that the teacher's behavior should change, too!

The problem is that neither the teacher nor the child can manage to use a different option. If a teacher is sending your kid to the office every day or giving him endless detentions that go nowhere, it means the teacher also doesn't have a workable alternative on tap.

In this case, the teacher is doing the only thing he knows how: getting the kid temporarily out of the classroom for some respite, while hoping the child will calm down or otherwise be in better shape when she returns. This doesn't mean the teacher is a bad one (yes, I know those exist—heck, ask any experienced teacher and you'll find out about at least one hair-raising past or present coworker). But it does mean that folks are losing sight of the real goal, which is to have a child who actually can behave better.

Illogical Consequences

Because kids with SPD aren't always able to do what they need to or to "behave" in a given situation, punishments and consequences can be counterproductive. There are such things as inappropriate, illogical, or just plain unjust consequences, and when a kid has SPD the chances of those occurring can multiply rapidly.

If, for example, you have a sensory-craving kid who acts up in class, a lot of times he might be held back from recess. Problem is, if he needs directed movement and activity to calm down, and a nice structured game of "red light, green light" will do that, you've just shot yourself in the foot. The extra time stuck in enforced inactivity will make the kid squirrelly and more likely to cause trouble during or after recess.

On the other hand, if you have a child who is not functioning well socially and is bullied because of SPD, keeping him in from recess will feel like a reward. I cannot tell you how great a relief it sometimes was to not be out on the playground!

You can't always get good behavior through standard consequences. When punishment becomes part of a pointless cycle, it's time to try to solve the actual problem.

My mother did that when she got me that alarm clock. While she was upset that I was wretched to deal with when I first woke up, the real issue was that she needed me to get out of bed at a given time. The alarm clock got her the results she needed when punishing me didn't.

See, I'm not necessarily "all there" when I wake up, so I lack the level of functioning that would enable me to behave in my own best interests first thing in the morning. I knew, absolutely knew, that taking on my mom in a fight was not the smartest thing to do. I knew that yelling at a person who is just waking you up is not kind or even sane.

But I didn't have the ability to change my behavior until I was alert to the world, so my mom got me an alarm clock that I could hit, slam, and generally be cranky at without hurting its feelings.

That was a non-punishment. It didn't change or reduce my responsibility, which was to get up and get ready for school. It didn't make getting me out of the house easy—that was an exhausting task even without my rage upon awakening. But it solved one problem and allowed me to be competent at one stage of getting ready for school.

Don't be afraid to use crutches when punishments and rewards just aren't cutting it. Don't be afraid to give support or assistance to a kid just because his behavior is "bad."

If a kid can't sit still in class and eventually starts rocking his chair back and forth or chewing on non-food items, like his shoes or another kid's pencils, then enforcing consequences may seem like a natural thing: He's destroying property and distracting the teacher, so he has to sit in "time out" or stay in for recess or … well, you know the drill.

The same kid, given a purpose or a set physical activity, might not need to get punished at all. If he likes to chew on stuff, maybe he needs something appropriate to chew on—they actually make "chewy fidgets" that are bits of tough, knubley plastic that are designed for chewing.

If that particular little boy (or girl) can't sit still, make sure he has as-signed physical tasks. He could help take the chairs down off the desks first thing in the morning, clap the erasers, or move books.

There's also a process that is called "antiseptic bouncing." (That's one of my favorite bits of insane jargon. No one could figure it out without being told what it's supposed to mean.)

"Antiseptic bouncing," translated, means getting the kid out of a situa-tion before he blows. He is "bounced" out of the situation or classroom. The "antiseptic" part comes from the idea that this is a preventative approach. Or else it's just something someone came up with to be deliberately obscure.

Bouncing a kid can work. He's starting to rock back on his chair, the teacher or aide calls him over and hands him an envelope, and she asks him to take it to the office, or the library, or wherever. This gets him moving and out of the room. He's not bugging other students, he's not endangering himself, and he's not driving the teacher batty, he's just going for a walk.

In a pinch, you can keep that going: Send the kid to the office with an envelope with a note that says, "Keep him moving," or some code phrase like, "The blue dog sleeps beside the purple hippo," or something. That cues the office staff to send him with another envelope to the library, with an order to bring back a response, and so forth.

Okay, that could get kind of ridiculous, but the basic principle is sound: An ounce of prevention is worth a mighty many pounds' worth of cure.

There is one barrier that can get in the way of non-punishment solutions: While there are brilliant behaviorists out there who are able to use the latest and greatest in behavioral psychology to motivate and help kids, there are a lot of laypeople (and even some professionals) who see behavior as black and white, with no shades of gray. An inflexible philosophy of behaviorism is not a pretty thing to face.

It can be painful for the rigid "behaviorist" to use non-punitive methods. They figure that if the kid is acting rowdy and you bounce him or otherwise keep him physically occupied, he'll never learn to behave—or, worse, he'll misbehave more to get the desirable outcome of getting to take a quick break.

These folks really do want to get good results, and usually they have absolutely no vested interest in thwarting a child. They just aren't keeping track of the whole situation. Maybe they are a teacher with umpteen other kids with umpteen other issues to deal with, or a parent who is fearful that "coddling" might make her kid grow up less than strong enough, or a therapist who has seen a lot of stuff but has too many kids to deal with or too little time. Or it could just be somebody who has been successful with a specific way of administering consequences so many times that it's really hard for them to let go when it isn't working this time.

Okay, once in a while it's someone who is just plain problematic. There are people who get stuck mentally, and there are people who need to be "right" so badly they resist anything that might show they were wrong. For this person, trying a new technique means risking having it work, and the level of anxiety they experience when that possibility rears its head is sad. If you can get your kid away from this person, do.

But behavior isn't all about punishment. Rewards and positive experiences often have a much greater, much more lasting effect than punishments. Neither way is always right, but going positive is a good first step.

Why is this? Well, for one thing, humans are creatures of habit. The best predictor of future behavior is relevant past behavior—there's a ton of research on that. So to get a kid to do something differently, you need to get that new and different behavior started.

You don't teach a dog to sit by yelling "Sit!" and wapping him on the head with a brick. You teach a dog to sit by holding out a treat, and as he starts sniffing it, you move the treat forward and over his head so he automatically sits on his butt to keep his nose on the treat. Then you say, "Sit," and give him the treat.

You keep tricking that puppy into sitting, giving him the treat, and eventually he associates the action with the word and happy time. Eventually you can phase out the treat, so you can reserve treats for learning new tricks, but that link between the word "sit" and sitting down has been created and stays there.

Heck, if you want your dog to stop overreacting to people when you go for walks, you just plain don't drag him away from people by pulling the leash until you choke him or by using a nasty, big, pointy, sharp chain collar or a shock collar. When you see a distraction coming, whether it's a person or a dog, you immediately DO something that is a better distraction. You could turn around and start walking another direction, or you could start running your dog through his tricks while holding out a treat

("Sit. Lie down. Kill a trial lawyer. Good dog!") and then rewarding him with said treat.

Any time you can prevent a dog from developing the habit of freaking out over people or other animals, you are able to grain into his mind the habit of responding to others in a non-freaked-out way. You pick an alternate good behavior and induce it. Punishment is too confusing, unless it's a super-short correction—like a brief tug at the leash that doesn't hurt him, but lets him know he needs to pay attention to you.

People also function better with praise and reward-based training than with punishment-based training. Punishment is sometimes useful, but if it's the only tool in your toolbox, you are not going to get the best out of other humans. Including kids with SPD.

The reality is that when you have a kid who can't sit still, he often will have developed specific habitual behaviors. It starts out with the shifting in his seat, moves to tipping his chair back, and then progresses to tipping his chair back and slamming it forward hard to make a great deal of noise and commotion. If you just punish him at stage 3, he's not learning new habits—he's just learning that school sucks, life sucks, and you hate him.

So do it differently. The kid who is sent on an errand or given a chore when he first starts shifting around is a kid whose "wind up" has been interrupted. It gives him a vital chance to learn that step 1 doesn't have to go on to steps 2 and 3—something his brain hasn't had a chance to pick up on.

If you've got a kid who is physically rowdy, you can teach him new habits that involve doing some kind of physical activity early in the day to start burning off that excess energy and get his brain and his body organized.

And once he's got some serious physical activity in his life, and he's used to some kind of bouncing, you can start getting him to the point where he is the one who bounces himself—where he can tell he needs a break and asks for it. That's a skill no human should be without.

So, while I am all for kids getting consequences, I do not believe that punishment is the One True Way of making kids better.

Independence and Consequences

But here I am, back to the whole idea of consequences. Kids do need to have a realistic idea of how their own negative behaviors (or lack of behaviors) can hurt them, or it will often come back to haunt them. For both long-term and short-term independence, kids need that clear cause-and-effect process to be part of their lives.

This means you look at the kid you have, how he really is now, and base consequences on what he is able to do and what his limitations are.

You do not, generally, make a kid who finds "slimy" foods nauseating handle or eat gelatin to punish him. You do not use a gym whistle to signal a kid who has seriously sensitive hearing, or make a kid who has poor muscle tone from years of severe under-responsivity drop and give you twenty. That just doesn't make sense.

Similarly, you don't use actual punishments for stuff kids can't help. You may let them experience natural consequences, because rushing in to rescue your child every time something goes wrong is the road to disaster, but you set the bar appropriately for that child.

You don't tell a kid with hemophilia that he should just clot already and then take away his dessert if he doesn't. You get him needed medical attention. You make allowances for his limits.

But, Boundaries, Man!

And yet, you do need to put those boundaries there. I gotta keep harping on this, because there is a distinct subset of humans who believe that if a child is "disabled," that child needs to be protected, shielded, and cosseted at all times. "He's special, he's a genius, he can't be expected to do these things" is a cop-out, and a dangerous one.

I was confronted once by a parent who was all but in tears when she told me how incredibly difficult her son's OT, speech therapist, and teacher were being. They kept telling her that her son needed to develop skills for independence, and, she told me, "I do everything possible to let him be independent, but first they tell me he should be independent, and then they get angry when I make sure he is."

The devil was in the details: She told me that to make her son more independent, she left his favorite foods in easy reach and never made him eat at mealtimes. She let him choose his own bedtime and TV shows. She let him have free reign at home.

She was an extreme case of not understanding that independence is built through age- and ability-appropriate challenges and boundaries. She didn't realize that letting her son do what he wanted wasn't going to make him, as a 6-year-old, learn to be independent, because life is not based on doing whatever you choose, but in being able to accomplish what you need to do.

A 6-year-old is not going to figure out that his listlessness is caused by a poor diet, nor that the reason school is awful every minute is that he's going on 5 hours of sleep a night.

Our kids have enough problems with foods and sleep without putting that responsibility on them. Allowing a kid to skip foods he cannot tolerate is necessary to prevent every meal from being a misery, but he still needs to show up for meals and learn to not to tell other people what he thinks of their food. Allowing a child to go through a soothing nighttime ritual or to use physical activity to organize himself for bed is cool—allowing a child to take charge of his own sleep schedule is not cool.

Emotional Self-Management

Emotional self-management, self-control, the ability to not lose it over life in general, these are all hard things for human beings to learn. It can be extremely difficult for a child who is struggling with SPD to get a handle on these tough skills.

We all expect that a child will have a certain amount of "maturity" at a certain age, but most kids don't get much coaching on actual concrete ways to deal with life maturely.

Kids who are obviously bright or who have one or two great splinter skills (like excelling in reading or math) are often called "mature" even while they work overtime to avoid physical and social situations they don't know how to handle.

Kids who don't have the splinter skills that would enable them to look "clever" (or who lack confidence in general) often inadvertently adapt by fitting into a stereotype that lets them off the hook. They may be perceived as *cute, hapless, shy, silly,* or *rough and tumble.* They don't lean on those traits in a purposeful or calculated way; these are coping techniques that develop out of sheer desperation, anxiety, and confusion. If looking "dumb" makes the stress and pain go away, even for a little while, the child winds up repeating those dumb-kid behaviors without thinking about it at all.

A stressed-out, anxious, or depressed kid will very naturally develop habits that act as short-term solutions, even though those habits may cause adults to think the child is lazy, slow, or deliberately manipulative—but a kid who is overwhelmed by SPD-related problems is generally *coping*, not con-niving. If they learn that a specific kind of misbehavior will keep them inside at recess, they might not even notice that the worse they gets teased at recess, the more they rely on that kind of misbehavior to keep them inside and safe.

The Biggest Problem

Powerful emotional states are, by nature, hard to manage. Sensory pro-cessing can be stronger and more urgent than any kind of logic, especially logic that comes from outside the child—like a lecture about how she should be feeling.

For example, a child with a really overactive gravity sense will often experience gravitational insecurity—the feeling of being in danger because of height and position. The feeling of gravitational insecurity outweighs any logic, explanation, or reassurance you can give a child. This is even more pri-mal than a phobic relation. You can't talk someone out of what their senses assure them is real.

Similarly, some children have an audio sensitivity that affects their response to sad-sounding music. Any dirge-like song in a minor key can make them feel overwhelming sadness. This can have odd side effects: Some children are scared of church because of the music—an organ can make vibrations that increase the intensity of this response.

In my case, a mix-up at my school resulted in me being placed in a fourth-grade math class at the time I started third grade. By the time I was reassigned to a third-grade class, I had missed a lot of basic multiplication, which meant I learned the times tables exclusively from *Schoolhouse Rock*.

The songs for the times tables for the numbers 8 and 9 on *Schoolhouse Rock* were so upsetting to me that I would change the channel or left the room. "Figure 8" filled me with sadness and despair, and "Naughty Number

9" terrified me. This meant I never could bear to pay attention to or remember either one of them.

I kid you not when I tell you it took me until I learned algebra to be comfortable with the times tables for 8 and 9, because algebra taught me to break down multiplication into numbers I already knew. So the associative, commutative, and distributive properties saved my neck when my audio processing tripped me up.

Human beings in general have strong emotions that can overwhelm their logical and emotion-management skills in specific sensory environments. Even in my current, significantly more awesome state, there are things I am pretty sure would affect me—and maybe you, too.

For example: I am a relatively pragmatic person. When I run across silly TV shows (and they are very silly) about looking for ghosts in old "haunted" buildings, I think things like, "Hey, do the guys making this show know this is totally fake, or are they sincere fakes?"

I mean, c'mon, they're using random scientific instruments in a dark basement at all hours. That ain't what I would call "reality."

BUT if you put me in the basement of a dark, creaky house that I've never been in before at 1 AM, I'll get pretty darn scared. I know there are no ghosties or ghoulies or long-leggedy beasties, but my senses will still react as if there were. It makes sense: A strange, dark place full of weird noises should trigger an automatic fear reaction, because there are parts of my brain more concerned with keeping me alive than with precision responses. After all, from a survival standpoint, being freaked out and unable to sleep is far less dangerous than failing to be ready for fight or flight in a situation full of unknowns.

Strange places, strange sounds, and not having any knowledge of what is actually there can give people with super-duper good sensory integration uncontrollable emotional reactions.

The difference with SPD is that a child can be having that type of reaction in a space that everyone else can tell is perfectly safe.

The point here is not to imply that it is impossible for children with severe SPD to learn emotional self-management, but rather to say that they are facing an uphill battle. They really need trusted adults who are willing to coach and support them, celebrating their victories and accepting their failures as part of the process.

Budding young SPuDsters are seldom able to guess their way to good self-management. The adults around them need to provide the clues.

Giving Credit Where Credit Is Due

When we are coaching kids to overcome the natural fear, panic, or other unhealthy negative emotions that stem from SPD (and from being a kid), we need to give them credit. You need to give your child and/or the child in your classroom and/or the child in your office the credit he deserves when he's working really hard for you.

I was once working with some OTs at a local school: I was there to provide them with information on Asperger's and autism, and they were showing and telling me about their work. There were two therapists in training who were just getting started and eager to learn. It was a great exchange with a wonderful group of people, and they were very encouraging with the children they worked with.

But everybody has moments when they forget basic facts. Late in the day, when both therapists and kids were somewhat flagging, I watched two OTs working with a child who had severe gravitational insecurity.

They had, through some miracle, convinced the boy to climb a ladder to a platform about 4 feet off the ground and were trying to convince him to take the risk of jumping onto mats that must have been about 8 inches thick.

There were two people there to help catch and guide his fall, and the mat was huge, surrounding him so it would be almost impossible for him to miss it.

He was, naturally, not so sure. He stood back from the edge, then peered over, looking at the 4-foot drop.

I saw his face. I knew what he was feeling. His face showed clearly that he wasn't seeing a short leap onto a padded surface. As he so very bravely dared to look down, what he saw was a dark and cavernous pit that would surely swallow him alive. (If you feel like don't understand what this could feel like, try checking YouTube for a clip of the dolly zoom from Vertigo, in which we see the tall spiral staircase from the point of view of someone with a severe phobia of heights.

One of the trainee OTs said, "Oh, come on, it's not that high." She was tired and frustrated, she had been up until all hours studying, and she forgot to apply what she knew about gravitational insecurity to that kid's situation. She didn't see what I saw—but then again, she'd never had SPD.

The correct response when a kid is attempting to summon his courage in the face of amazing, overwhelming fear is, "I'm so proud of you for getting up there."

I was very proud of myself that day. Despite the fact that an occupational therapy gym area always has some decent blunt objects around, I did not smack that young women upside the head with anything. I responded to the situation in a nonviolent way. Clearly, I'm doing well these days.

Also, the kid jumped. And he got the applause he deserved.

Cognitive Whodewha?

Chapter 13

I was going to give this chapter a title that indicated it is going to be about the cognitive components of emotional, social, and practical self-management, but then I realized that the reaction of a typical reader might well be, "Huh?" There's potential for a lot of jargon in here, so I'll try to keep it to the more obvious material and provide good explanations and translations into the kind of language humans actually use.

SPD can obviously cause specific sorts of physical pain and distress. There is the pain of the oversensitive child, which can occur in any one sense or combination of senses. There is the physical stress caused by a poor diet or lack of sleep. There is the exhaustion and frustration experienced by the child who is clumsy or has little strength and can't participate in games and active play. All of these things can be addressed through encouragement, through occupational therapy, and by creating a supportive classroom environment where the child is not penalized for his neurological problems.

There are a lot of ways to modify activities, environments, and expectations to help a child get from point A to point B with less physical distress and discomfort. We can provide a sensory diet, useful activities, and a wide variety of momentary helps and interventions, like weighted toys, heavy work assignments, or a safe retreat that provides a sensory break. It may take a while to find the right combination of activities and approaches, but it is usually possible to make a lot of headway toward giving your child with SPD a life with less pain and physical stress, as well as a greater ability to learn and keep up with other students.

But the pains, problems, and struggles of the person with SPD (and humans in general) actually have two parts: the physical part and a vitally important emotional and mental part.

The physical part is more straightforward, and is not too hard to tackle from the outside. The emotional part is trickier, but just as important—sometimes even more important than the physical. Emotional states such as panic, anxiety, hopelessness, anger, and self-downing actually make physical pain feel worse. It's not a trick, nor an illusion: The brain perceives pain plus stress as intensified pain.

Of course, emotional and mental pain can arise without any physical pain being involved. Strong feelings and thoughts like anxiety and self-downing can cause serious problems even when there isn't physical pain involved. This is true both when there was never any immediate physical distress stemming from the child's SPD in a given situation and also after the physical pain has been eliminated from the specific situation.

This means that recognizing the stress, emotions, and mental habits that develop in a child with untreated SPD (or with SPD combined with other factors) is very important. Children and adults with SPD often find themselves in situations where the most natural thoughts that occur in response to their experiences are not only negative, but factually inaccurate.

Take for example the case of a child who has sensory under-responsivity, so much so that it takes her a while to notice when it's time to take her book out during school. The teacher tells the children to take out their books, but with low or slow audio responsivity this particular child takes a while. All of the other children have pulled out their copies of *Mildly Interesting Cultural Differences of Many Lands* and have progressed from following along on page 41 to following along on page 42, but poor Esmerelda has just noticed that quiet reading time is over and lesson time has begun.

The practical part of the problem is fairly simple: Esme has missed part of the lesson and needs to catch up. This is definitely an annoyance to Esme, but it's the kind of problem the people around her can easily help her solve.

The emotional component is a bigger problem: Esme feels like she's an idiot. For as long as she can remember, she has thought, "Why can't I do what the other kids do? Why am I always behind? I must be really dumb. *All* of the other kids are *always* smarter than me."

The adults around her can fix the practical component one way or another. If her parents are willing to help her, or if the school has a tutoring program, she can catch up on what she missed while the adults had not yet figured out how to help Esme keep up with the class.

If her teacher or an aide taps Esme's shoulder or otherwise signals her at transition time, she can get on the same schedule as the other children. A bell or buzzer in the classroom can alert all of the children clearly when it's time to start a new task or activity. Even better, maybe vigorous activity in the early morning will get Esme revved up and ready to go.

With some patience and detective work, Esme's parents, OT, and teachers are bound to find activities that can wake Esme up and keep her on track. Her sensory under-responsivity doesn't need to be completely "fixed" to improve her practical situation greatly.

But what about Esme's habitual self-downing? It may well have become part of her usual routine, and could recur any time she finds herself getting behind. It may be such a firm habit that it persists even on days when she keeps up.

Even when things are going well, there are bound to be things that get in the way of Esme's new way of doing things. What about days when she's just gotten over a cold (or is coming down with one) and finds it hard to engage in physically alerting activities or games? What about substitute teachers who don't know they need to alert her, or don't think it matters? What about days when things just aren't going well enough for any of this stuff to do the trick?

On these "off" days, Esme needs to have a few skills on hand. Thinking "I'm so dumb" is a really natural and normal reaction to finding herself consistently behind, the kind of thing any of us might automatically think. But it sure isn't going to help her catch up.

What thoughts would help Esme out here? What can she realistically say to herself that will work better?

If she's only told happy-happy thoughts to make her feel better, it can make things worse for her. It genuinely doesn't help to say, "You're not dumb, you're smart," or "You're so talented!" or "Of course you aren't slow!" or (the worst), "You could do so well if you tried a little harder!"

When a child has a lot of practice at feeling dumb, simply telling her how incredibly smart or talented she is won't build her up. She knows from experience that she has limits, and she may well know that people are saying something's wrong with her—hey, I knew that when I was in the second grade, and no one told me much of anything directly.

The key is that the responses and information Esme or any child with SPD gets have to be rational and realistic. They have to make sense to her—and no BS. That's key.

The child with SPD is not likely to figure out what kind of thoughts to come up with to help herself—heck, many adults don't know how to come up with self-helping thoughts in tough situations.

This is where parents, teachers, OTs, and pretty much anyone else who interacts with kids can help. Esme, like all of us, is pretty much on her own the moment that she feels dumb, and making a fuss over her or telling her how smart and good she is won't help.

This is where little kids need to know about big ideas. One of the biggest ideas that even kids who are pretty small can get a handle on is brain plasticity.

They don't actually have to know the phrase "brain plasticity."

What children do need to know is that their brains can become stronger and better. The human brain responds to things like studying and working out difficult problems by developing more and more connections in the brain—the brain actually gets better when you learn. I know!!!!

Not only that, but making mistakes and having them corrected actually makes you even smarter! As in, if children are given easy tests where they get everything right, they don't really remember much, but children who get harder tests where they make mistakes and have the tests handed back and reviewed remember far more. The process of striving, failing, and then succeeding is incredibly good for your brain! In fact, failing grows your brain.

Okay, okay, there are some things you might fail at that won't actually help your brain. If the phrase, "Start with the tequila," "KEG STAND!!!" or "Blindfolded, of course," are involved in an activity, your brain might appreciate it if you just walked away.

Official Science-Type Terminology: Mindset

There's a researcher, Carol S. Dweck, PhD, who coined the term "mindset" to describe two possible ways of seeing things. A lot of people have caught onto her work, and there is a lot of serious research showing that this mindset thing is a big deal.

Here's how it works: If you didn't understand that your brain can grow and improve with any learning activity at any age, you might well think of talent and smarts as something you are born with: Either you have it, or you don't.

That's one of the two kinds of mindsets that Dweck describes: the *fixed* mindset. The fixed mindset is the belief that you are what you are, period. In this way of thinking, the basic assumption is that you were born smart or not smart, talented or not talented, and the amount of smarts and talents you got at birth is what you've got to go on. Sure, you will sometimes improve at things, but only the things you innately have the ability for anyway.

The research says that the fixed mindset is especially common in kids who "fail to perform up to expectations." In fact, the fixed mindset makes smart kids not so smart!

While the fixed mindset is a rough ride and can occur in anyone, regardless of testable IQ, I'm going to go back to my favorite example here: me. (You knew it would come back to that, didn't you?)

Actually, in this case, saying I'm my "favorite" example is incorrect. I'm not thrilled at all to be sharing this, but it's kind of important to get this concept clear.

I was a "smart" kid. I have no idea what happened. I'm not nearly as smart as an adult as I was at age 6.

In first and second grade, I was the kid who finished every worksheet first and made no mistakes. I ripped through phonics, addition, and subtraction like nobody's business.

Yeah, I can still do phonics, too.

And, of course, I wondered why I was fastest and the other kids often took a long time to do the same exact worksheets. The answer was, of course, that I was a smartie. I was intelligent and clever and academically talented.

Oh, I was so gosh-darned awesome it was amazing. My parents would go all nuts when I used big words correctly at the dinner table, read books above my age level, and basically any time I did my super-smart smartie thing.

There was a special pattern to the praise and reinforcement that came with being an smart-smart smartie. What really impressed the adults was when I did things effortlessly, as if they were no big deal. Oh, yeah, it was brilliant when I read The Mini Page in less time than it took my dad to read the comics, or when I knew clever quotes or obscure facts. (For those of you too young to remember, the Mini Page was/is a children's feature in dead-tree based newspapers. And, as previously indicated, get off my lawn.)

The thing that made my (supposed) smartness matter was that it appeared out of nowhere and involved no visible effort on my part. I haven't been able to do that effortless genius thing in about, oh, 40 years now, but when I had it, it was sooooo cool.

What the adults around me didn't realize was that I was learning a hard-and-fast rule (which, I think, affected my sister heavily as well). The rule was, "Intelligence and talent are effortless and come naturally, without you having to do much of anything."

The corollary, which any kid would deduce easily, was, "The kids who take a long time, make mistakes, or otherwise struggle are clearly not special smart-smart super-smarties like you. Poor things."

This way lies madness. I just happened to have the skill to do certain bits of schoolwork without feeling like I was working or struggling—up to a point.

But, of course, I hit a point in school where I couldn't just do the work without effort. It hits different kids at different ages, but everyone gets there eventually. What's worse, it happens in different subjects at different times, making the child feel like they are losing it bit by bit.

The kids who had been taking, I don't know, a few minutes more than I did to complete their worksheets—they were learning to learn. They were working on their reading or math skills, making mistakes and fixing them, asking for help. Yes, sometimes they gave up, and some of them didn't get very far because they, like me, imagined that intelligence was something they either had or didn't have. Those poor kids thought it was no use to try.

And so did I. I thought it was no use to try. I was terrified of seeming stupid or inept. If "smart" was effortless and natural, then struggling could do nothing but show how dumb I really was.

If you don't do your worksheet, if you procrastinate with all the power you possess as you agonize over your own toxic self-doubt, if you just plain won't try, then no one can prove that you are dumb. A blank worksheet is the result of laziness or procrastination, remember? No evidence of "failure" there.

If you believed you were as smart as you will ever be and that struggling would prove you weren't smart at all, you might well freak out and panic. There might be a tiny little bit of anxiety involved as well.

You may remember from an earlier chapter that I struggled mightily with my guitar and with comic books—things I loved but just didn't "get." For some reason, in areas I didn't think of as being academic, I was perfectly comfortable with having to work to make progress. In fact, when, through hard work, I found that I had little to no talent, I kept working. It was interesting to learn and there was always the chance I'd make a little more progress.

Maybe it was that the myths were different. The (false) myth is that Einstein flunked math when he was young—as if his genius only burst forth later. Better to do badly and be a potential Einstein than struggle and be seen as hopelessly mediocre!

(**Note:** Einstein excelled in math at a young age, doing calculus at 11. He also got a doctorate in physics before he wrote his papers on relativity. He worked a boring and difficult full-time day job while working on his revolutionary papers at night. Yet the idea of him being an "outsider" who did badly in school as a child is a myth that appeals a great deal if you have the fixed mindset, where genius just emerges from people spontaneously.)

Fortunately, the myths I knew about the music world were actually true. The myth and legend was that the Beatles worked their collective rear-end off to become the musicians they were, the musicians who had the skills and experience to write and perform hit after hit, amazing album after amazing album. These were guys who worked for chump change in incredibly difficult conditions for an awfully long time. They were also people who practiced and honed their skills. The classic "played my first guitar 'til my fingers bled" story is genuinely true of the late, great George Harrison. So I figured hard work was part of learning music, period.

Because I actually had many examples of stories about musicians who had to work hard for a long time to become good at what they did, I didn't see failure as failure. I mean, the only way to know if you could play music would be to practice a lot and try again and again. The fact that I failed even when I worked really hard just meant that I wasn't talented at everything. It was a bummer, but not devastating.

In other words, when I learned real stories about real people succeeding, it turned out that most of them needed to work hard to succeed.

But my experience of seemingly effortless smartie smart smartness up to age 6 or 7 grained into my brain the idea that intellect was either there or not. The fact that when I suddenly and spontaneously did well in certain subjects—Algebra was my good friend—I got lots of praise and even actually impressed my dad meant that my idea of instant smartness or none at all got heavily reinforced.

In fact, I read all sorts of random things for fun, and I therefore occasionally could just bust out a bit of knowledge or knowhow for a specific task that was way ahead of my age group, and that meant getting that sweet, sweet, fixed-mindset style praise. Oh, I lived for that.

Meanwhile, when I was just not performing up to expectations, which was a lot (see pretty much every report card of mine for proof), I was told, "You're so smart, you could do it if you just tried." And I tried, and I struggled, and then I knew I wasn't smart. But if I pretended not to care, and maybe somehow pulled a bit of brilliance out of thin air ("thin air" meaning voluminous, constant reading), maybe I would get to feel smart again. At least for a little while.

Did I mention that I think the fixed mindset worked against me when I struggled with SPD? Oh, yes.

The Other Mindset

Since we know that the brain is an amazing organ that actually can grow through learning and struggle and get better and better, there has to be a mindset that goes with that reality. That would be the growth mindset.

The growth mindset is fact based and is a great help to kids with SPD, as well as to those who feel dumb, and to kids who, like me, felt dumb and then smart and then dumb again 10 or 1,000 times a day.

Why is the growth mindset so important to kids with SPD? Because it tells us that your brain can grow new cells and new connections, and thus become progressively more awesome. This means that every person with SPD can overcome some or most of the problems and pains that come with their particular expression of SPD.

The connections and processes in the brain that take sensory input and make it into information can be improved, and then they can be improved again. All of that occupational therapy or speech therapy, all of the heavy work and active play, all of that stuff helps brains to grow and mature.

As a child, I knew that some areas required work for growth, but I didn't understand that *everything* the brain does can be improved. I thought working hard was evidence of failure and limitations.

Your child needs to know that there are many activities that help children's bodies and minds develop, *and* that the hard work of schoolwork helps their brains grow and develop.

This means your child should know that being behind and struggling because of SPD doesn't doom him or her to being behind forever. Every child's brain can grow through learning.

Your child (or you) might reasonably point out that there are children who are intellectually disabled or who have other problems that often limit what they are able to do. That's true; we certainly haven't yet reached a place where we know how to take all children and make them experts in theoretical physics *and* auto repair *and* social niceties.

It's true that humans have limits. The "you can be anything" idea that is ingrained into so many kids is just not literally true, and kids who are thoughtful often figure that out.

What your child needs to hear from you, loud and clear, is that getting better is good, and doing your "personal best" is a real achievement. From any starting point, pushing your limits and growing a little more than you thought you could are great accomplishments!

When a child thinks she is "dumb" because she has SPD and has therefore had a lot of experiences that make her feel "dumb," then she needs to know: Not only is every human being born with some degree of intelligence and talent, but every human being can develop that intelligence and talent through *work*. Sometimes it's hard work, sometimes it's fun work, sometimes it's both. Sometimes it's just rote practice of boring things, like times tables and spelling words, so you can develop a basis for learning more important and engaging things as you gets older.

What to Do

So do tell your child, at whatever level you think he can get, anyone at any time can start getting smarter and better at lots of stuff. Let him know that even though everyone has days when they don't do all that well, they can keep improving.

Also, praise your child for making an effort and for taking the kinds of risks that help her grow. No, I don't mean risks like jumping off the roof—I mean trying things that are difficult, or trying again after a nasty failure.

Dweck and others have tested various things to say to children to help them develop that growth mindset. It has been pointed out that the kind of praise and the statements they suggest can seem odd, but sometimes normal just doesn't cut it.

Instead of "You did well, you must be smart," say, "You did well, you must have worked hard."

Instead of "Wow, you did those problems really fast," say, "Wow, that was so easy, it was kind of boring. Let's find something interesting to do instead."

Seriously, that's an important thing to say to your child: "That was easy; that was boring."

Other recommended phrases include, "Hey, what an interesting mistake," and "Oh, I just made a mistake, let's figure out how to fix it."

And what's a kid to think when she's lagging behind or frustrated at school because she has SPD? How about, "Hey, I'll get there. Tortoise and the hare, baby!"

Or, "Well, sometimes I do dumb things, but so does everybody. Even really smart people do dumb things sometimes."

Or, "Wow, this is a pain. I wish it wasn't so hard, but I can do it."

My personal favorite thought, the one that got me through K-12 with my sanity intact (questionable) and a halfway decent grade-point average (for sure) was, "Well, this worksheet/test looks hard, and I'm pretty sure I'm gonna tank, but I might as well see if I can do some of it. I mean, if I put down everything I know and do as much as I can, at least it probably won't be a zero, and it will be less boring that just sitting here doing nothing."

Logical and functional thoughts don't have to be happy, cheery, perfectly peppy ones. What many kids can use is rational, realistic ideas, like, "Well, I'm not as smart as I can be quite yet, but I'm working on it." See if you can help your child develop more of a growth mindset, so he or she has a chance at having rational thoughts to help him through the day.

W hat every story and idea in this book has in common with every other is an attempt to find practical ways to think differently about kids who have SPD. Diagnoses, accommodations, and therapies are great tools, but they all come from and succeed because of parents, teachers, and others who are able to think about the child they see in front of them in a new and more sympathetic way.

It can be incredibly hard to get beyond the basic idea that "What you see is what you get" when we observe other humans. When someone is making you crazy, you see them as a problem. When a child does something that makes you feel frustrated or manipulated, the normal reaction is to assume the child is purposely being manipulative and is doing so merely to aggravate you.

In reality, the world is full of people who have many different reasons for how they behave, including differences in what they know, how they perceive what is happening, and what they are actually capable of doing in the moment.

One last story to explain how important this is.

Call me nutty, but when I'm driving, I hate to get cut off, hate being tailgated (especially in the right-hand lane!), and hate hate hate when another driver does something that makes me hit the brakes or otherwise take evasive action.

I spent a lot of years in traffic getting mad at people. In fact, I sometimes have gotten mad enough that I get a certain satisfaction out of being pointlessly controlling; for example, I may feel happy that I am blocking someone who cut another guy off because he "deserves" it.

At some point, between the reading and the research and learning to take more charge of my own emotions, I realized that getting angry wasn't helping me. It might feel good momentarily to be indignant and look down at another person who is driving in a non-ideal manner, but it wasn't getting me anywhere.

And I started to de-fang my road rage. I started playing a game whenever anyone cut me off or was trying harder than I thought he should to get where he was going extra-fast. The game was to list all of the reasons why the other driver might be doing stuff like that.

He's late for work.

She's late for a job interview.

She didn't see me.

The kids in the back seat distracted him.

They're on their way to the emergency room.

She really, really needs to get to a rest stop.

They can't afford the charge for picking their kids up late from daycare.

She's supposed to get a call about medical test results any minute.

He's had a lousy day, so it's good I'm driving defensively so he didn't get hurt.

Of course, there are things drivers do that are actually not okay. If a driver is clearly driving while intoxicated or dangerously distracted, that's not good, and may even require me to get on the phone to report a dangerous or out-of-control driver. But seriously, how often does that happen?

If someone is driving less-than-perfectly, I make the effort to not take it personally (most of the time). I take it as the result of any number of factors that have nothing whatsoever to do with me, and that means I stay calmer. If someone else's driving is suffering due to circumstances, then keeping my own cool to the best of my ability is my best shot at being safe and avoiding hurting myself or others.

It is sometimes rough to pass up the chance to feel self-righteous. There's a quick hit of feeling good that comes from feeling superior and judging others. But giving up on feeling superior feels really good in the long run.

Of course, there's a lot less positive feeling in judging children to be doing bad things, being deliberately mean, or being habitually lazy. Those things aren't actually fun to think about. It's no particularly enjoyable to say, "You could do it but you aren't trying," or "It's like you're *trying* to drive me crazy!"

The point—the Hokey-Pokey core of this book—is that if you can get your brain and your child away from the idea that you can judge children by their appearances at all times, you can help your kid and even maybe get to keep a small sliver of your own sanity.

That's one of the two things I really wanted to say. The other thing is, "Thank you."

After I've dragged you through so many personal stories and chunks of information about SPD, what it's like to have SPD, and what can be done to help children with SPD develop skills and confidence, I want to *thank you* so much for coming along for this ride with me. That "thank you" applies whether you've read every word avidly or have read a few bits here and there and have wound up at this bit of the book randomly.

Thank you for being curious. Thank you for wanting to learn. Thank you for not just wishing your child, or your student, or you, could be better and stronger and more capable, but for being willing to put time and energy into working toward that goal. That goes double—no, TRIPLE—if you, like many people out there who are helping kids with SPD, are overloaded and frazzled a lot of the time.

Thank you for your time and energy. I sincerely hope you got an insight, an idea, or a slight bit of a smile from what you've read. I hope to have given you a few helpful bits of information that can help with the difficult process of learning to see children with SPD differently.

And yes, I know, not every answer is here. Not even close. There are not enough pages here to cover all of the aspects and expressions of SPD—or, at least, not until my editor caves and agrees to let me publish my beloved 20-volume epic novel, *The Amazing Team of Adventurers with SPD and the Magical Caravan of FanFic*. Apparently there's a problem with getting the rights to all of the characters from *Star Trek*. And *Star Wars*. And *Buffy the Vampire Slayer*. And *Tiny Toons*.

Oh, and one more thing: Sometimes when people hear me telling these stories at conferences, they come up to me afterward and say they are so sorry I had to go through the experiences I did growing up. I'm not sorry at all. I'm here, you're here, and maybe there's something useful that could come from it. That's all that matters.

That's what it's all about.

Great Books on Sensory Issues

The Out of Sync Child

by Carol Stock Kranowitz, MA.

This is the most popular book on sensory processing disorders and well worth reading for any parent. Note: I had a parent tell me that she'd read it and "Not all of the suggestions were good for my kid." That's always going to be true, because SPD varies so much; read this (and all of the other books recommended) with that in mind.

Sensational Kids

by Lucy Jane Miller, PhD, OTR

Everything and more you might want to learn from the foremost researcher for SPD (who is also the foremost advocate for kids with SPD). Lots of info on diagnosis, treatment, coping methods and advocacy.

No Longer a SECRET

by Doreit S. Bialer, MA, OTR/L
and Lucy Jane Miller, PhD, OTR

This book is tops for ways to inexpensively and effectively create supports for children with SPD. It also has great, specific information on how to help children with specific SPD subtypes.

223

Building Bridges through Sensory Integration

by Paula Aquilla, BSc, OT

This book covers great ways to identify and address sensory problems. While the book often focuses on autism, the material will be helpful to any parent, teacher, or OT who works with any child who has SPD.

DVD set: Sensory Strategies to Improve Communication, Social Skills, and Behavior

presented by Paula Aquilla, BSc, OT

A three hour presentation that provides concrete information and examples for working with any child with SPD. Great explanations of how sensory problems can affect behavior and how to help children focus and learn.

Great Books On Related Topics

We Said, They Said: 50 Things Parents and Teachers of Students with Autism Want Each Other to Know

by Cassie Zupke

This is a vital book about why and how parents and teachers get into conflicts and what each side really needs to know about what the other is trying to do. All parents whose kids with teachers (and vice-versa) need to read this book. Also, it's incredibly readable and not too long. Keep a copy on the back of every toilet in the house.

How to Teach Life Skills to Kids with Autism or Asperger's

by Jennifer McIlwee Myers, Aspie At Large

This book covers techniques that work for any child through grade school and even beyond, and talks about the importance of teaching skills that allow a child with SPD to function better and with more confidence. Also the writer is a total babe.

Mindset: How We Can Learn to Fulfill Our Potential
> by Carol S. Dweck, PhD

Behavior Solutions for the Inclusive Classroom and More Behavior Solutions for the Inclusive Classroom
> by Beth Aune et al.
> Beth is a genius when it comes to creating these easy-to-use books that allow you to look up specific problems and find solutions.

The American Physical Therapy Association Book of Body Repair & Maintenance
> by Steve Vickery and Marilyn Moffat
> A great book with lots of drawings that allow you to see how the joints and muscles work and how the body can and should move.

About the Author

Jennifer McIlwee Myers (the middle name is "Mac-uhl-wee") found out that she had Sensory Processing Disorder at the time she was diagnosed with Asperger's Syndrome in mid-2002, and has focused on studying and conveying information about both SPD and autism in the years since. Jennifer currently writes and lives in sunny Southern California with her husband Gary and, at any given time, a cat or two.

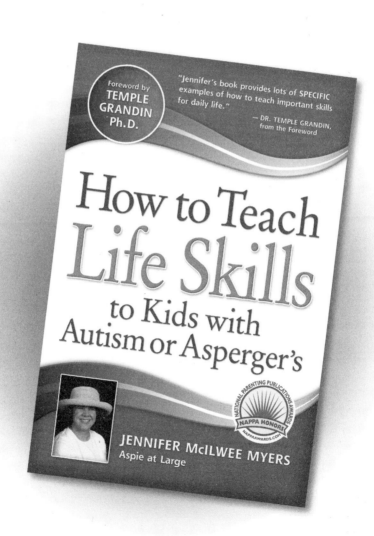

Introduction

Temple made me do it.

After years of giving presentations on various aspects of the autism spectrum, I'd had many, many people ask why I didn't write a book about autism and Asperger's Syndrome. Various publishers and authors had suggested various topics, and I actually had three different books underway. My normal level of disorganization is such that they all were growing but not getting much closer to being finished.

Then I called Temple up one evening in June of 2009 about something completely different, and she asked what I was working on. I mentioned that I wasn't really sure what to write about or which book to focus on.

"Your life skills talk," she told me, "you need to write a book about that."

I started to protest that I already had started other books and wanted to finish one of those, but she cut me off.

"Your life skills talk is good, that's what people need. You need to do an outline from that."

For roughly the next hour, she walked me through the topics in my talk, while I frantically scribbled notes on bits of scrap paper. She gave me strict instructions for creating an outline based on those topics.

Finally, she told me, "Get the outline to me by Tuesday morning so I can tell you whether to go ahead with it."

It was Sunday evening.

I got the outline to her by Tuesday morning.

1

She approved the outline and I started going. The result is the book you are holding in your hands.

The moral of the story is to not ask Temple for help unless you really want her help, because she doesn't mess around.

Thank heavens.

So this book is based on my various talks about life skills, which means it is written more or less the way I speak. Grammarians take note: this means the language use is casual, with plenty of non-standard usage. This means that sometimes the awkward but correct use of "he or she" and "his or her" is replaced with the incorrect but readable "they" and "their." The usage changes with the flow of the language, just as it would in a talk. Also, there are sentences that start with "so," "but," or "and," which is also going to drive the grammarians nuts but is, again, really quite normal in speech.

Additionally, this book contains quite a number of asides or quick references that are based in geek-think. Don't worry if those asides don't completely work for you: they aren't vital to the meaning of the text, but they may make things a little clearer to my fellow geeks. Consider them tiny shout-outs to my fellow Aspies, and if you aren't into the "geek world" you can just let them pass.

Thanks for reading this. And yes, I am aware that I owe Temple big-time.

— JENNIFER MCILWEE MYERS

Why You?
Why Me?
Why Life Skills?

Hi, my name is Jennifer and I'd like to provide you with tons of information, hints, and ideas about how to teach life skills to children, teens, and/or humans with autism spectrum disorders.

I have Asperger's Syndrome (AS), which is an autism spectrum disorder. That alone certainly does not qualify me to teach you or anyone else about Asperger's and autism, but getting diagnosed with AS turned out to be the starting point for a journey that led me here, to you, and to the hope of sharing with you what I've learned on that journey.

In addition to having AS, I am an extraordinarily lucky person, and my incredible amount of sheer dumb luck has led me to experience and discover a lot of great stuff about how learning life skills can greatly enhance not just the lives of children with autism spectrum disorders, but also the lives of those who live with them, care for them, and teach them.

You are, I hope, a person who would like to understand more about teaching, reaching, and helping someone with an autism spectrum disorder. Or you may just be someone who got stuck in the bathroom and this is the only thing in there to read.

Parents and teachers of children on the autism spectrum have a huge ability to affect that child's functioning in the world. A parent or caregiver who is willing to take on the job of teaching life skills can lift that child to his or her best possible level of functioning in the world.

Not all of us on the spectrum are destined for greatness; nor are all of the children with autism who struggle actually "secret geniuses" who will blow the world away with their brilliance someday. But we are all human beings who need to be able to get by from day to day with some small measure of independence and strength.

I hope this book will help you to move yourself and your child towards better day-to-day functioning. I really, really, really hope that it will give you some insight into how people with autism think and feel, and what it is we need extra help to learn.

At the very worst, if you are stuck in the bathroom with this book, and after you wash your hands, you find there are no dry towels in the bathroom, you might use this book to blot them on. Glad to be of service.

WHY LIFE SKILLS?

There are so many things involved in parenting any child, and so many things for a child to learn in order to function as an adult: the alphabet, how to ride the bus, calculus, frugal shopping, putting on one's own socks, and deciding whether you should or shouldn't change your own oil.

The problems and tasks of parenting often are doubled or tripled when a child has any autism spectrum disorder (ASD). Suddenly, parents have to face the ins and outs of IEPs, figure out what exactly an occupational therapist is and whether their child needs one, and determine which of the many proffered treatments are mad, bad, or just plain dangerous.

So why should parents (or teachers, OTs, speech pathologists, and psychologists) put "teaching this child life skills" high on the list of things to deal with? How can anyone make time for life skills when so many children with ASDs are woefully behind in academics, speech, or social skills?

What's more, many parents have hopes or fears that make life skills a low priority. Many tell me that their child either is or is soon going to be "cured" and therefore doesn't need special intervention for day-to-day skills. Others fear that their child is so low-functioning, so hard to educate, that there is no point to trying to teach him to do laundry, make a simple meal, or even pick out his own outfit in the morning.

But no matter where a child is on the autism spectrum, and no matter where he or she is likely to wind up, life skills count!

Yes, there are children with autism (and people in general) who may have little chance at being independent in later life. But there is a huge difference between an adult with autism who is used to being waited on hand-and-foot and one who is able to get dressed on his own, help with the dishes, or successfully use simple stress-busting techniques.

Similarly, no matter how smart a child is, or how "recovered" he may wind up, if he can't go out to lunch with the guys from work, choose his own outfits, or deal with other people's mistakes calmly, he's going to wind up living in a very small, sheltered world.

Not only are people with ASDs less likely to pick up skills like this on their own, but we also take a lot longer to learn them. Simple exercises like crossing the street or taking the bus may be completely non-obvious to us, regardless of IQ. And learning how to deal with mistakes calmly and appropriately takes us a long, long, long time. Heck, I'm forty-four, and I'm *still* working on it!

The nature of schooling and our society mean that children are often judged and ranked by their academic skills. But there are jobs you can hold if you can't read. There are jobs you can hold if you can't write. There are even jobs you can hold if you can't talk.

There are few or no jobs you can keep if you yell or scream when you don't get what you expected. There are very rarely jobs you can hold if you can't stop talking when your boss is trying to tell you something. Being on time and being dressed right for that activity are so important to employment that being late to or dressing badly for an interview are job-killers.

Sure, a few people get away with yelling, being late, dressing wrong, and so forth—if those people are such huge money makers that it is worth it for folks to put up with them. But even super-geniuses will have an easier time getting on with life if they learn a few basic skills.

And even kids who will probably never be independent adults get more respect and more support if they can do the little things that inform the people around them that they are human beings. A guy who has occasional meltdowns but mostly understands the idea of doing his fair share and of apologizing for causing others pain or inconvenience is simply more likely to be treated with a modicum of respect and friendliness than one whose behavior constantly triggers defensive responses from those around him.

Even social and support groups that are specifically for adults with ASDs have to have standards. A group that includes people with super-sensitive ears, noses, and hearts is not going to be happy to include people who yell, smell, and raise hell.

THE GEEK WORLD

Many parents and teachers, even some with very high-functioning children, believe that there is not much out there for a child with autism. They feel it is okay to skip teaching skills like functioning in a grocery store, doing household chores, and other daily tasks, because they believe their child is always going to need constant daily care.

This makes sense only if you think the socially oriented "neurotypical" (NT) world is the only real world there is. That's the world that most elementary school teachers, occupational therapists, marketing executives, and a disproportionate number of women inhabit.

In the NT world, *Star Trek* fans are geeks, and people do things like stocking up on greeting cards and buying gifts for no occasion "just in case" something comes up and a gift is needed. That same world involves a wide variety of behaviors that I find rather incomprehensible, from the use of decorative towels and soaps that cannot be actually used to (shudder) "manscaping."

These are the folks who enjoy dinner parties and social dancing, who believe that every opportunity for schmoozing is good, and who, given the choice, choose work that brings them into contact with other humans most of the day.

These people naturally come to believe that the child with autism—the child who prefers solitude to clamor, who loves to focus on one problem or activity for hours at a time, who loves organizing objects infinitely more than organizing social activities, and who has no innate urge to attend a playdate—well, they come to believe that this is a child who will never find a way in the world.

What these folks don't know is that there is a whole world of us already out there. It's the geek world, and it's hidden right under their noses.

Yes, one of the most vital reasons that children on the autism spectrum need to learn life skills is that there is a whole geek world out there waiting for us to find it. The kinds of skills that are discussed in this book are the ones that make it possible for us to find, interact with, and develop lives in that world.

And yes, the geek world is real and valid. There's a reason that Temple Grandin refers to NASA as a sheltered workshop for people with high-functioning autism. There's a reason that some people's work cubicles are decorated with action figures and *Doctor Who* calendars. There's a reason that Hollywood can make a killing off of elaborate boxed set releases of *Lord of the Rings* that have twenty or more hours of behind-the-scenes extras per movie.

This geek world is almost invisible to "typical" parents, teachers, therapists, and peers. It is the world of engineers, computer programmers, research scientists, animal experts, writers, artists, and many others. It's a place where the "geeks" hang out, and it exists both within and in parallel to the one where you who are typical live.

There are college dorms full of engineering and science majors where every other person will love trains. There are break rooms at NASA where arguments about the relative merits of comic book superheros are de rigueur.

It's not just the "brainy" geeks who can benefit from living, working, and making friends in the geek world. Model train clubs, Lego™ clubs, and other special interest groups often are places where kids who can't fit in anywhere can fit in.

Heck, I live in Orange County, California, USA, where we have a thriving Lego Model Railroading club. That's right, a club for people who like to build model train sets out of Legos. Not incidentally, this is a club founded, run, and populated by adults who can afford to buy their own Legos. Thousands and thousands of Legos.

Parents of the most introverted autistic children often despair of ever finding a way to draw those children out. They might find a way by venturing into the geek world as it exists near you. Folks who love model trains may be able to help you figure out how to work trains into all of your child's social-skills and life-skills training.

Children and adults who are considered "low functioning" can really benefit from contact with people in the geek world. The world of a teen or adult who is obsessed with Thomas the Tank Engine™ can be greatly expanded by adults who speak the language of trains.

Most important, I want you to know and remember that there are grownups—functioning, employed grownups—who have massive doses of the traits associated with the autism spectrum. This is one of the most vital reasons that teaching life skills is important—because we geeks, wonks, and nerds are living fulfilling lives throughout the world. People with autistic traits who learn to be polite, hardworking, and generally functional have the best chance to join in. It can be done. We exist. There's a whole world of us out there.

Please teach your child the life skills needed to join us.